Alister L. Mackie

THE TRADE UNIONIST
AND
THE TYCOON

The Trade Unionist
and
the Tycoon

ALLISTER MACKIE

Foreword by TONY BENN

MAINSTREAM
PUBLISHING
EDINBURGH AND LONDON

in conjunction with

First published in Great Britain in 1992 by
MAINSTREAM PUBLISHING CO. (EDINBURGH) LTD.,
7 Albany Street, Edinburgh EH1 3UG
in conjunction with
THE HERALD
195 Albion Street, Glasgow

A catalogue record for this book is available from the British Library.

ISBN 1 85158 515 X

Typeset in 10 on 12 pt Bembo by Origination, Luton. Printed in Great Britain by Butler & Tanner Ltd, Frome.

Dedicated to the memory of
Jimmy Russell and Charlie Armstrong

Contents

Acknowledgments

IT WOULD be difficult to the point of foolhardiness to attempt to give due acknowledgments to all those who aided me in compiling the book. Many played a crucial role in the task unbeknown to themselves. For example, the original idea of writing a book was not mine – it was Robert Maxwell's.

During the final few days of my chairmanship of the newspaper, Maxwell gave instructions that all the Action Committee minutes were to be located so that he could commission a history of the struggle. It was evident that any such account would be likely to border on fiction and be written from an angle calculated to enhance Maxwell's role. This could not be allowed to happen. If there were to be a book it would have to be as objective as it could. This was, and remains, my perceived debt of honour to those who were courageous and at the same time generous enough to invest in our dream, in particular our own workforce; or those politicians and civil servants who declared their support for us and worked in our interests in the background, all the while inevitably harbouring genuine doubts about our chances of survival.

So I removed all the Action Committee minutes, and there were volumes of them, painstakingly hand-written out by my long-standing friend and colleague, Lawrie Hooper. I smuggled them out of the building bit by bit, aided and abetted by another anti-Maxwell activist, Tommy McGhee.

Since I was the sole person in the organisation who knew the whereabouts of the minutes, I managed to carry out my task under everybody's noses and during the course of a single day while Maxwell was actually organising the search. Having completed that part of the operation, I then went through the files of every member of the Works Council, extracting the minutes of the Works Council meetings. Finally, I selected from the correspondence files every letter which I deemed to be of any significance. With the sole exception of my own Works Council minutes, I then fed all of the others through the shredder so that only I, I believe, had a record of the business of the Works Council since the start-up of the paper. Thus no history of the *Scottish Daily News* could be comprehensively written unless it was done with my consent and co-operation.

But having naively manoeuvred myself into this particular cul-de-sac, I found myself soon to be pushed into attempting to write the history myself – a task for which I have neither talent nor training. However, to me the book had to be far more than a historical account; it also had to be an exploration of how a group of working-class activists think and react in such circumstances. It had to be an honest account, including the glory and the weaknesses that emerged.

All through the book, written during the winter months of 1975/76, when my memory still vibrated with the events, I have sought total honesty, even about my own shortcomings. To do otherwise would surely negate the intention of the book. If I have misrepresented or strayed from the straight path of absolute verity, I say in earnestness that I regret my failing and offer my profound apologies. All steps have been taken that can reasonably be taken to be totally objective, knowing all the while that total objectivity can be no more than an intention and never a reality.

So, finally, I would like to acknowledge my appreciation of everyone involved – the workforce whose decision to set up a co-operative inspired the book; posthumously to Robert Maxwell whose intention to have the book written in the first place compelled me to write this account, and whose passing allows it to be published free from the fear of writs from him; Lawrie Hooper, whose meticulous minutes made the whole thing possible; Richard Briston and Jimmy Russell, whose continual hectoring galvanised me into writing the book; and Arnold Kemp who undertook the task of editing it. Having made all of those acknowledgments, and realising that many more names remain unmentioned but are every bit as much appreciated, I feel it must be obvious to the reader that my own contribution was no more than one of allowing myself to be the medium through which the book wrote itself: the story comes through me, not from me.

ALLISTER A. MACKIE
Bathgate,
December 1991

Foreword

THE STORY of the *Scottish Daily News* is one that will long be remembered in the Labour movement because – along with Meriden and IPD – it was one of the very few attempts made by workers to transform a collapsed capitalist enterprise into a working co-operative to save jobs and transform the nature of their work.

But the *Scottish Daily News* was the only one which received the unwelcome attention of a rich, ambitious and crooked man – Robert Maxwell – who believed that he could turn this new co-operative into a money-spinner for himself.

This book is about the struggle for survival, and for power, between the workers and their would-be new boss, posing as their saviour.

It is indeed a riveting story, brilliantly written and wonderfully documented from the papers collected at the time and safely smuggled out of the building by its author, Allister Mackie.

I first met Allister and his team, in Glasgow, in May 1974, within a few weeks of becoming Secretary of State for Industry in the Labour government that had scraped home without an overall majority, that spring, and I expressed my personal support for what they were trying to do, knowing how hostile my own colleagues, my civil servants and the Treasury would be to what was proposed.

We had taken over from the Heath government after the miners' strike which he had precipitated, and almost immediately I discovered that several huge companies, such as Ferranti, Alfred Herbert and British Leyland, were on the point of collapse, and we never knew from day to day whether we could survive, as a minority government, in a hung parliament.

There was also a major internal battle going on inside the Labour Party between those of us who were committed to the radical manifesto upon which we had been elected, and the majority of the Cabinet who had no intention whatever of implementing our election policies and wanted to damp down all such expectations.

My own political situation was therefore almost as uncertain as it was for the Albion Street workers, whom Allister was representing.

I was determined that those workers who had become victims of the economic crisis should be assisted in every way possible to weather the storm and come out with control of their own future in a new framework based upon some pattern of industrial democracy, and that public funds should be made available to make that possible.

Two visits to the offices of the paper in Glasgow served to confirm my own commitment to their project, although during the second occasion Maxwell was there and he tried to turn it all into a publicity stunt for himself.

Never in my long political and ministerial life have I encountered such violent opposition as there was against the co-operatives.

The Treasury, which had happily provided enormous sums of money to bale out private companies, was resolute in arguing against even the smallest grants to the co-operatives, and the City saw that if they were allowed to develop then the ultimate sanction against trade unions and workers – which was the sack – would lose its sting and the bosses wold lose their most powerful disciplinary weapon.

The Industrial Development Advisory Board, composed of industrialists, reported against all my recommendations, and later that year my Permanent Secretary tried to report me to the Public Accounts Committee for the misuse of public money – which got me into a lot of trouble with Harold Wilson.

The trade union leaders were equally unhelpful because trade unions – as they saw it – were there to bargain with management, and not to set up some new management structure of their own.

I was indeed summoned by the then General Secretary of the TUC, Len Murray, and rebuked for giving a small grant to the Wales TUC to do some research, without his permission, and the delegation which he led to see me about the *Scottish Daily News* was obviously embarrassed at what it had come to say and was therefore unconvincing.

But so strong was the public support, at that time, for the policy which I was following that those who wanted to prevent it had to set up absurd legal and financial hurdles which they hoped would prevent these new enterprises from getting off the ground.

This was the method used when the *SDN* prospectus was presented to officials to examine and the ministerial committee laid down impossible financial targets before any public money would be released.

Allister realised what was going on and at a fringe meeting organised by the Institute for Workers Control at the Labour Conference on November 27 1974 at which he and I spoke he said: "If ever you are to have workers' participation in the newspaper industry, it can only be by complete control by the workers, so that the working-class point of view can be put across", and in winding up I highlighted this very point myself.

In the event, when the paper did appear, though it had dropped the right-wing Beaverbrook bias, it lacked the sharp political cutting edge that I had hoped to see and of which Allister had spoken.

But it was the very fact that the *Scottish Daily News* was a newspaper that caused the most bitter opposition of all, for the control of information is the most powerful of all the powers that the establishment wields, and they had no intention of seeing it weakened.

It was for that reason that Harold Wilson, who knew my views on the media, had specifically transferred responsibilities for the press from the Department of Industry, which I headed, to the Department of Trade under Peter Shore, not realising that the only source of funds that could be used were those under the Industry Act which I had to administer, and that was why I was able to take the lead.

As the deadline, set by the Treasury for the raising of the money through the prospectus, neared, I feared that the target could not be reached and that all the work done would fail, and, on March 27 1975, I was just about to send a bitter minute to the Prime Minister complaining that he had killed the paper, when I heard from Allister that Robert Maxwell was putting up extra money.

I had known Maxwell for over twenty years, before, and during, his time as a Labour MP and had distrusted him from the first for his devious and dishonest way of dealing with those he thought he could use to advance his own ends, and this book contains the most detailed evidence ever of exactly the way that he worked.

But he did have the cash to get the *SDN* off the ground and although I knew that he was only interested in getting his foot in the door of the newspaper business I had some confidence that Allister and his colleagues would be able to defend themselves, as they were.

The final stages of the conflict described so vividly in this book will probably remain as the best account ever of the nature of the man who lied and cheated his way to the top and was ready to destroy anyone who stood in his way, using his wealth to serve intimidating writs on anyone who ventured a word of criticism against him.

In the end the *Scottish Daily News* died and Allister lost his job again, I having been sacked earlier that year by Harold Wilson for – among other things – the support I had given to workers in a struggle.

Looking back on it all nearly twenty years later this story may seem to have ended in tragedy but history does not always work out quite like that, for we are back in the deepest slump since the 1930s, and it will reawaken some of the radicalism that was crushed out of us in the greedy eighties, and the blatant bias of the newspaper proprietors – not to mention the Maxwell scandal – will surely require us to look again at this industry and how it is run and controlled.

I remain as firmly convinced as I was then that the idea of a workers' co-operative running a newspaper, or a broadcasting station, offers us the best chance of avoiding the twin dangers of government or commercial control of the media. I salute Allister Mackie and his work in chronicling the problems they had.

Those who set out to do it again may find my diaries, for the same period, equally revealing for they show that the forces ranged against any such attempt were formidable and determined and we shall have to find a way of overcoming them too.

TONY BENN
27 June 1992

Introduction

THIS REMARKABLE book first came to my attention in the late seventies. At that time I was deputy editor of *The Scotsman* and was on the lookout for interesting material to serialise and (or so the idea went) increase sales. A search of this kind is not quite as strenuous as looking for the Holy Grail but material of sufficient originality and interest to extend the circulation of any newspaper, especially a serious one, is not much easier to come by.

The first thing I noticed about Allister Mackie's manuscript was that it was exceptionally well written. My second observation was that he had composed it almost as if it were a novel, with frequent use of direct speech. My third was that Allister, though he at no point conceals his utter distaste for Maxwell, does not spare himself and his colleagues when he deals with the various equivocations they had to use in order to secure his investment in the co-operative they had formed to publish the *Scottish Daily News*. My fourth reflection was that the book, for all its merits, raised very serious problems. At the time they proved to be an insuperable barrier to its publication and the chief among them was Robert Maxwell's litigious nature. The dilemma was that had the book been emasculated to make it safe from Maxwell libel writs, it would have lost the qualities that made its publication worthwhile.

Now after all those years it has seen the light of day. It has taken Maxwell's death, in mysterious circumstances, to make its publication possible. It retains, perhaps to a surprising degree, its freshness and interest. The episode itself has been well documented already in *The Story of the Scottish Daily News* by Ron McKay and Brian Barr (Canongate, 1976). Allister's account is personal and even partisan. Though it is remarkably fair to Maxwell in many ways it does not purport to be an even-handed account. But because it is first-hand evidence, it casts light on a moment in Scottish labour and press history in a way that a more consciously balanced history could not. From it we can draw many conclusions about the attitudes of an industrial class at a point in Scotland's economic history when the country was embarking on a period of such rapid and profound change that the skilled working class, of which the *News* caseroom was so interesting an example, would face its own progressive extinction. The political and social consequences of that period are everywhere apparent today. New technology has transformed and is transforming the publishing industry. The irony of the co-operative was that it was formed to save jobs in areas where techniques were being profoundly changed. Perhaps that was really why the enterprise could not succeed, although the rest of the industry was not to embrace the new technology until the eighties. Change of this kind can be deferred but cannot be denied for ever. In that sense, the episode in Albion Street so vividly described here was a milestone on the road to the tragedy of Wapping, when Murdoch confronted and defeated the London print chapels. In its own time frame, as the book makes clear, the paper was a great success from the standpoint of production. Its production manager, Jim Roy, is still at Albion Street where together we are colleagues on *The Herald*, he as night production manager, I as editor. He and the rest of the production staff are the heroes of *The Trade Unionist and the Tycoon*. Allister's verdict is uncompromising: the journalism was inadequate. The newspaper industry is a curious one. You can set up a perfect production process but if you have nothing to say then you might as well forget it. Comparable industries, I suppose, are to be found in the arts, like cinema, or in the fashion trade where without the flair of the designer the textile mills will ultimately grind to a halt.

For most people, however, the chief interest in the book will come from its portrait of Maxwell. Since his death we have seen the full extent of his criminality, yet in his lifetime he bullied, charmed and beguiled quite sensible people whose chief fault was that they were more keen to take his shilling than honour should have allowed. Allister and I have in common the fact that we were both recipients of a Maxwell writ. He can boast that his was for a million while mine was merely for half that. I had the good fortune that BBC Scotland, and its then controller, Mr Pat Chalmers, were staunch in their defence of me after I had made some contentious remarks about Maxwell's prosecution of an industrial dispute at the *Daily Record* in 1987. Allister was not so fortunate. Scottish Television settled with Maxwell and left him to face the music alone. As the outcome showed, Maxwell used the writs as a means of shutting his critics up, for in both our cases he settled for a pretty mild statement. In my case, I published a paragraph saying that "if it could be construed" that I had impugned his integrity, I would of course regret it. Pat, the judge, counsel senior and junior, and all my fellow hacks who had keenly looked forward to seeing Maxwell in the witness box were disappointed: Pat had to be consoled with a glass of champagne which I stood him happily: in my judgment, we had won.

In the book we see the character traits that were to lead Maxwell to grand larceny of the Mirror Group pension fund. Here we see a lack of frankness amounting to mendacity, a gift for manipulating funds, a tendency to make spurious promises about available resources. But there was more to Maxwell than that. Some of his commercial ideas were perhaps not as daft as Allister and his colleagues thought at the time, though their reasons for a generalised suspicion of everything he suggested remain perfectly understandable.

What makes the narrative fascinating, however, is the conflict of personalities that lies at its heart. Allister is a Scottish Labour activist of the old school. His culture is rooted in the old socialist idea of improvement through redistribution of resources and universal education. Lenin gave up British socialism as a hopeless cause because it was too rooted in religion, and much of the Christian framework of Keir Hardie's socialism survives in Allister's attitudes, just as his prose makes the occasional biblical allusion. His conflict with Maxwell was inevitable not just because he put the principle of the co-operative per se above the commercial interests of one large shareholder. I suspect that Allister, whose own progressive and growing comprehension of commercial principles is an interesting thread in the book, could have done business with such an investor had he been a man of principle and trustworthiness.

The Thatcher era was punctuated by a series of City and commercial frauds which have largely gone unpunished. I suspect that in a different climate Maxwell might not have raided the Mirror Group pension fund with such freedom. He was a rogue elephant, as Allister remarks at one point in the book. A rogue elephant living in the age of the City rogue is liable to go even further astray, and that perhaps is what happened to Maxwell. The judgment by the Board of Trade inspectors that he was unfit to run a public company has been amply and sadly confirmed. It remains a great surprise that he managed to fool so many people. He seduced and beguiled the *News* workforce by a black mixture of lies, bullying, fear and charm. Allister fought him tenaciously but was eventually unable to counter him. Even in his own peer group, Allister found himself almost alone. The Labour Party has a record of subservience to Maxwell which it is now doing its best to forget. In the eighties Maxwell duped many people who ought to have been able to see through him if they had adhered to their professional principles as so admirably did many of the legal and financial advisers who served the *News*. That is another story, and one that will not be fully told for many years.

In editing the text I have been fortunate that the original was in such good shape. The mails between Glasgow and Bathgate have been busy during our co-operation. As I worked on the text, I could feel the pace of the narrative quicken as it hastened towards its inevitable denouement. It has something of the quality of a psychological thriller. I am delighted that it has at last achieved the publication which it has for so long deserved, and I commend it to the reader.

ARNOLD KEMP
The Herald,
Glasgow, 1992

Prologue

IT WAS the afternoon of Tuesday, November 5, 1991. I was helping out at The Big Apple, a fruit and vegetable shop in Whitburn, West Lothian, which I had helped to set up some 11 months previously, when the phone rang. It was Ken Bryson from BBC Scotland. He told me Robert Maxwell was presumed dead.

I provided what seemed an appropriate response, going through the motions of regret but with no great conviction. It was not until later that evening that the impact of the news began to reach me. True to form, his death was adorned with a mantle of mystery. He could never have walked quietly into the night. His death was always destined to be different from that of mere mortals. He was gigantic, monstrous, a man who made up his own rules and then broke them when it suited him.

He it was who at one time pervaded my life. No man I had ever met had made such an impression on me or had influenced my outlook so much. I knew no hatred for him, only a scant respect for his ability to convert his greed for power into the reality of power. My experience with him in the newspaper industry left me scarred but unhurt, a wiser but unembittered man.

At a later stage he sued Scottish Television and me for one million pounds. His action followed a television interview in which I severely criticised him and his style of management. It took place at a time when he had handed out redundancy notices to the entire staff of the *Scottish Daily Record* and *Sunday Mail*. It was evident that the workforce were heading for a rough passage. My statement was no less than a declaration of support for them. I said among other things that although he called himself a socialist it should be borne in mind that Hitler, also, used to call himself a socialist.

At the time I was leader of West Lothian District Council with an income which scarcely allowed me to provide for the basic needs of my family. To make matters worse, I could not claim legal aid since none is available in actions for defamation. The minimum cost of engaging legal help was estimated at around £20,000. However, with the help of John Teague, a local lawyer, and Mary O'Connors, an extremely helpful official at the Court of Session, I managed to cope.

After a time STV did a private deal with Maxwell, leaving me on my own. In the weeks before I was due to represent myself in court, he surprised me by sending me a personal letter in which he almost begged me to apologise. In particular I had attempted to draw, he wrote, a parallel between himself and Hitler. He protested that this comparison, "in the circumstances of what my family suffered at the hands of the Nazis, you must have known would be particularly offensive and distressing." In the end, and at the eleventh hour, a mild letter of apology from myself satisfied him sufficiently for the action to be dropped.

Had the case gone ahead my basic defence would have been to justify my comments rather than to apologise for having made them. After all, I reasoned, did not his conduct while at the *Scottish Daily News* justify my opinion of him? I had made up my mind to challenge Maxwell's statement line-by-line and word-by-word, even to the extent of demanding conclusive evidence that he was, indeed, the holder of the Military Cross. When I had first met him and learned of his being a former army captain and a holder of the MC, I had doubted both claims. Journalist friends had investigated the records and could find no reference either to his commission or his decoration. When I asked Maxwell for hard evidence, he unconvincingly claimed that both his commission and his award had been conferred on him in the field of battle; thus neither had been processed through traditional channels.

At a very early stage of my relationship with him I had asked him how he came to bear the name of Maxwell. He gave me what seemed a perfectly logical explanation. He had volunteered for the Army with no preference for any regiment. In due course he appeared before a recruiting officer who advised him, firstly, to change his name from Hoch to something more British lest he be captured by the Germans and exposed as a Czechoslovakian Jew; and also that he be enlisted in a regiment removed from the front line to lessen the chances of his being taken prisoner in the first place.

According to Maxwell's own account to me, he agreed to both suggestions. On the first, he chose to adopt the name of the recruit immediately in front of him – he was a Scotsman by the name of Robert Maxwell. On the second, he agreed to enlist in the Royal Artillery and he left me with the impression that he had served there for the duration of the war.

Maxwell's simple account seemed borne out by a totally independent and surprising source a few years later. I was attending a dinner representing the district council. Our hosts on the occasion were the Automobile Association. Seated next to me was the owner and managing director of Lindsay's of Edinburgh, a printing and publishing firm. We discovered we had a mutual acquaintance – Robert Maxwell. He told me a strange story. In May 1945 he was serving as a major in the Royal Artillery and was then stationed in Berlin. It was a time of chaos and disorder. The German Army had surrendered and with its going there was a breakdown in law and order. There was anarchy on the streets. The British Army did its best to restore some sort of order but had problems with some of its own troops. There had been sporadic looting and systematic black marketeering. My publisher friend was on duty as Arresting Officer one morning when he was instructed to report to another detachment there to arrest a group of artillerymen who had been caught red-handed in a black-market racket.

In the group there was a sergeant who seemed to be in charge. He was Sergeant Robert Maxwell who now claimed to be Captain Robert Maxwell, MC. He was duly court-martialled, found guilty, and sentenced to serve six months in the glass-house subsequent to his dishonourable discharge. In my companion's opinion, there could be no question of mistaken identity. Had he not almost lived with him for weeks on end prior to the court-martial? Like Maxwell, he himself was a printer and publisher. He wished he could arrange a confrontation with Maxwell which would allow him to challenge him. But that confrontation was never brought about, for my dining companion died suddenly.

Who and, more appropriate what, was Maxwell were questions we frequently pondered in the Action Committee and Works Council. That he had business acumen was never a matter of dispute though nearly all his practical suggestions were injudicious and would have harmed our company. Russell and Briston, arguably the two best financial brains in Scotland at that time, were convinced that his role among us was to destroy us. The evidence, I was forced to agree, pointed to no other conclusion. From then on our discussions centred on the reasons for his actions.

At first I believed he was motivated by a scheme to take over control of the newspaper, following its inevitable collapse, for an investment of just over £100,000 – a good return for so paltry an investment. This theory certainly seemed to be borne out by the collapse of authority of the Works Council and his subsequent assumption of office as chief executive. But when he did attain his objective, he simply hung around for another three weeks, doing nothing to help the paper. Indeed, he seemed to make its demise more certain by removing from effective leadership those who might then just have still saved it. Then he bowed out, leaving the workforce to the inevitable disaster, leaderless and beyond hope.

Why did he behave in this manner, why did he walk away from the scene when he had attained, almost, what we had believed to be his objective? Did he intend to destroy whatever faint chances of success the co-operative had? Had this been his motive all along? The idea of a newspaper controlled by a workers' co-operative became discredited to the point where there has been no major attempt to start up another in the 16 intervening years. Was this what he hoped to achieve? If so, on whose behalf was he operating? Was he financed from some other source? The suspicions grow in the recesses of my consciousness. The Treasury officials had an almost pathological hostility to our proposals. There was every bit as much from traditional communists. One union president and member of the Communist Party advised me we had no right to attempt to create an island of socialism in a sea of capitalism. His attitude seemed a nonsense to me at the time but perestroika in the USSR has revealed that there was apparently virulent opposition to enterprises such as ours within the Kremlin. And perestroika also revealed there was money paid to Pergamon Press by the Central Committee of the Communist Party.

These suspicions will never be put to rest. They remain in the mind and are lived with.

List of Chief Characters

(In order of appearance)

LAWRIE HOOPER: Secretary of the Beaverbrook Federated Chapel for nine years; *Express* stereotyper; secretary of Action Committee; company secretary of *Scottish Daily News* for a short spell.

CHARLES ARMSTRONG: Second deputy FoC (father of the chapel) of Beaverbrook Federated Chapel; *Evening Citizen* stereotyper; member of Action Committee; member of Works Council; now deceased.

JAMES McNAMARA: First deputy FoC of Beaverbrook Federated Chapel; FoC engineers' chapel; member of Action Committee; member of Works Council.

JOCELYN STEVENS: Managing director of Beaverbrook Newspapers; chief negotiator on behalf of that company with Action Committee.

DENNY MACGEE: Former FoC of journalists' chapel in *Express*; member of Action Committee; assistant editor, *Scottish Daily News*. Now deceased.

ALISTER BLYTH: FoC of *Express* stereotypers' chapel; member of Action Committee; member of Works Council; eventually chairman of *Scottish Daily News*.

NATHAN GOLDBERG:

Former *Express* journalist; member of Action Committee and Works Council; assistant editor, *Scottish Daily News*; promoted to editor.

BERT LIDDELL:

Former Natsopa *Evening Citizen* chapel official; member and treasurer of Action Committee.

TOM BAND:

Department of Trade and Industry Official based in Glasgow; now chief executive of the Scottish Tourist Board.

JIMMY RUSSELL:

B.Sc; former *Express* financial journalist; member of Action Committee and Works Council; now deceased.

JOE McGOWAN:

FoC of *Citizen* caseroom; member of Action Committee and Works Council; FoC of *Scottish Daily News* caseroom.

RONNIE GIBSON:

Former chapel official of clerical workers; member of Action Committee; FoC *Scottish Daily News* clerical chapel.

JIMMY CROSSAN:

FoC, electricians chapel; member of Action Committee; imperial father in *Scottish Daily News;* workforce representative on Works Council.

WILLIE RIDDELL:

Staffman *Express* caseroom; staffmen's representative on Action Committee; now deceased.

IRENE MACKAY:

Former clerical worker in Beaverbrook Newspapers; sole female member of Action Committee.

ROBERT MAXWELL:

Owner of Pergamon Press; member of Works Council; co-chairman and eventually chief executive of *Scottish Daily News*; now deceased.

RICHARD BRISTON:

Formerly professor of accountancy, Strathclyde University; financial adviser to Action Committee; financial adviser to *Scottish Daily News*.

MIKE CUDLIPP:

Formerly of *London Broadcasting* TV; journalist and technical adviser to Action Committee; engaged by Robert Maxwell.

GAVIN BOYD:

Senior partner of Boyd's of Glasgow, solicitors; legal adviser to Action Committee; legal adviser to *Scottish Daily News*.

BRIAN DORMAN:

Partner in Boyd's; legal adviser to Action Committee; legal adviser to *Scottish Daily News*.

ROY PATRICK:

Junior partner of Boyd's; legal adviser to Action Committee; legal adviser to *Scottish Daily News*.

ERIC TOUGH:

Formerly PA management consultant; general manager of *Scottish Daily News*.

BOB DALLAS:

Partner, French & Cowan; financial adviser to Action Committee and *Scottish Daily News*.

WILLIAM BARGH:

Former headmaster and Co-operative Movement activist in the Glasgow area; chairman of Investors' Council of *Scottish Daily News*. Member of Works Council.

DENNIS CANAVAN:

Labour MP; member of Investors' Council.

JIMMY MILNE:

General secretary, Scottish Trades Union Congress; member of Investors' Council; Member of Works Council.

WILLIAM WOLFE:

Former chairman of Scottish National Party; member of Investors' Council; company secretary of *Scottish Daily News*.

PART ONE
The early days

CHAPTER ONE

The roof falls in

March 17, 1974

IT WAS a warm, soft spring day, the sort that is compensation for a shift worker who can enjoy it. A short trip from home had taken me down to Linlithgow Loch with its ducks and swans. The midges had appeared for the first time that year. Their strange, darting dances above the water seemed a promise of good days to come. But the calm scene made me more introspective even than usual.

There was cause for worry in Albion Street, the Glasgow publishing centre of the *Scottish Daily Express*. I worked there, in the Bauhaus-style building clad in black vitreolite. I was a compositor and was chairman of the Federated House Chapels. The chapel is the basic unit of union organisation in a newspaper office and the Federated House Chapel was composed of all such groups in the building.

In its heyday the *Scottish Daily Express* had been king of the industry in Scotland. Lord Beaverbrook being himself of Scottish origin had kept a special warmth in his heart for it and had not stinted it for men or money. But the Beaver was dead. The paper's sales in Scotland had been overtaken by those of the *Daily Record*. The company chaired by his son, Sir Max Aitken, still traded under the name of Beaverbrook Newspapers. A thrusting young publisher, Jocelyn Stevens, had been brought in as chief executive, but the old man's journalistic genius did not seem to have lived on.

In Glasgow rumours abounded. The company, which also published the *Evening Citizen,* had been losing too much money and had indicated that it intended to "put things right." To me this meant one of two things. By then the *Express* was the only UK national still printing in London, Manchester and Glasgow. Either Manchester or Glasgow, it was expected, would have to close.

Denny Macgee and some of the other activists in the editorial chapel had, with the extravagant use of maps and the optimistic deployment of statistics, tried to persuade us that Manchester was doomed. Realists believed Glasgow was for the chop. If so, what could we do about it?

In only a couple of hours the speculation became reality. When I returned to my home in Bathgate, a BBC reporter phoned to tell me that Beaverbrook were closing Albion Street. Mentally prepared though I had believed myself to be, I was stunned. The printing operations were to cease on March 30. We had 12 days to find a solution and in the circumstances a solution seemed unlikely.

The answer, if there was one, had to lie in the Federated Chapel of which I had been chairman for some nine consecutive years. When I had taken it over it had barely existed and certainly had no teeth. Lawrie Hooper, then the clerk, and I had agreed there was a need for a powerful Federated Chapel which the management would have to respect and, more importantly, which individual chapels would learn to value. And over the years we had created exactly that – possibly the strongest federated chapel in any national newspaper in Britain at that time.

When I arrived in Albion Street that evening I immediately convened a meeting of the fathers of the chapels. The atmosphere was as intense as an electrical storm. I had nothing to offer them. I looked around as they waited for me to propose a "solution". They were all my friends, my dearest possessions gathered over the years. But they weren't necessarily the best men for the task of fighting the closure; and we would need only the best men. I had stumbled on the first step, at least. I would wind up the federated chapel and in its place form a small committee of the best men, not necessarily fathers of the chapels. It would be invested with complete authority without having to refer back its decisions to individual chapels. "It shall be called . . ." I said, my mind groping. And then I remembered a name I had come upon in a biography of John McLean, the Scottish revolutionary politician who had been a thorn in the flesh of the Government during and after the First World War. "It shall be called . . . the Action Committee."

It did the trick. This was the sort of instant action the FoCs had been looking for and it at least gave the workforce a feeling that the machinery was now in place to bring about the miracle of averting their looming redundancy.

THE FOLLOWING day Jocelyn Stevens came to address some of the workforce in the City Hall, round the corner in Candleriggs. Only chapel officials and various levels of managements were allowed to attend. Stevens, a golden-haired Adonis, perfectly dressed, was capable at times of arrogance and petulance. As he addressed the meeting it became increasingly obvious that the Glasgow management had known little or nothing of the plans for the amputation that had been laid and hatched over many months in London.

Stevens made it clear that the decision was irrevocable and beyond negotiation. There would be an orderly withdrawal to Manchester. The cream of the journalists would be retained by Beaverbrook in the Glasgow office or offered employment in Manchester. Other workers, but not many, would also be offered employment in either of the two other offices. The general workers, the non-craft workers and members of the Natsopa union, seemed to be coming out of it best of all. Already arrangements had been made to have some of them moved south. There would be good redundancy payments for everyone and the workforce would all be well-behaved, otherwise we would not receive all the money they had planned for us. The blackmail was laid on the table for us to mull over. Along with others, I left before the end. There was no point in listening when there was so much to be done. But what? Would the unions rally round on our behalf when most of us realised that the alternative to closing Glasgow seemed to be to close Manchester? It was already evident that Natsopa, at that time the strongest of the print unions, had already accepted the situation and, indeed, had done a deal with Beaverbrook to secure jobs for its own members.

The TV camera teams were waiting outside. Until that moment I had not fully realised the whole significance of what was happening to us. We newspapermen were now ourselves the news. In my interview I was very cautious but that night I received a call from Hugh Brown, a Glasgow MP whom I knew fairly well. He asked me how things were going and if he could help. After a short talk we agreed to meet. I cannot accurately recall the conversation, conducted amid the din of the caseroom. Yet I remember his words clearly. "Have you looked at the possibility of forming a co-operative?" At the time it seemed crazy but the idea grew in my mind because eventually there seemed no other.

THAT EVENING we formed our Action Committee of eight members. Apart from myself in the core group were Hooper, Charles Armstrong (deputy father of the federated chapel) and Jimmy McNamara (the other deputy father).

Hooper was tall and slim. A heavy beard made up for the lack of hair on top. "My head has been put on upside down," he used to say. Armstrong, the youngest of the officials, was abrasive, self-opinionated, aggressive, energetic. Like Hooper he was a stereotyper, a member of the department which cast plates ready for the rotary presses. He was handsome and dressed in the latest style. His glasses were always of fashionable design and, until you met him up close, gave a deceptive impression of easy charm. In fact he was as hard and unyielding as the streets of his native city. He was a Glasgow Catholic reared in the Protestant stronghold of the Calton and had in his youth joined the Young Communist League. He dealt ruthlessly with irrelevance in argument and trusted no-one until he had proved himself: then he would support him whatever the personal cost. He was made of iron.

McNamara, like myself, was totally politically motivated. He was a member of the Communist Party and received his industrial and political education in the shipyards of the Upper Clyde. An engineer, he was short, balding, bow-legged. He seemed forever dressed in boilersuit open to the waist with an oil-stained T-shirt underneath. We had been friends for more years than I could remember and he was my political confessor and mentor.

We had agreed beforehand that there would be no room for passengers. Denny Macgee would have to be a member. We all agreed on that. Not that we were anxious for his counsel. But if he were not on the committee he would become passionately hostile to it.

For years he had been father of the editorial chapel but had resigned two years before. During his reign he had been a thorn in the side of management. His tools were impassioned and theatrical rhetoric, hysterical arm-waving and synthetic indignation. Any other chapel might have laughed at him but the journalists swallowed it, and indeed seemed to be in awe of him. Once he boasted to the federated chapel: "I have destroyed two editors in my time; I wonder how many more there will be." Once he had been drummed out of the caseroom following a stoppage over a Cummings cartoon which showed a priest-like Brezhnev supplying arms to the IRA. Macgee, a Catholic, had raised such a hullabaloo that the paper was stopped. Macgee was convinced that his religion accounted for the caseroom's hostility (untrue because the caseroom FoC was at that time a Catholic). The real reason was it had grown weary of editorial's readiness to disrupt production. As an observer I had been present at the editorial chapel meeting to which Macgee had reported the incident of the cartoon. "I, your FoC, went into the caseroom and was greeted with terrible abuse. Alone I stood there (his right forefinger pointed to the ceiling), your representative, while being called a papist bastard. If I am a papist bastard then it is for you to say so." He pointed dramatically at his audience. "No, No, No!" came back the chorus of horrified voices.

The other three members of our Action Committee were Alister Blyth, Johnnie Burke and John Ferguson. Blyth, like Macgee, had been a problem for the company. Whenever the journalists had not been responsible for stopping production then it would almost always have been the stereotypers, whose FoC Blyth was. He was intelligent but introspective and brooding. Burke, the FoC of Natsopa, was an obvious choice not just because he represented the largest chapel but because we thought, wrongly as it turned out, that he had bull-like strength and determination. Ferguson, an advertising representative, was not an active trade unionist but was chosen because advertising was going to be vital if we were to create our own newspaper.

The day after Stevens's speech we met Jim Jack, the general secretary of the Scottish Trades Union Congress, at the same time seeking a meeting with the Prime Minister. Events were moving swiftly. On Wednesday we convened a mass meeting of the workforce. It was the biggest meeting ever held in Albion Street or, indeed, any other newspaper in Scotland. And I confess that I don't believe that I ever enjoyed addressing a meeting so much in my life. I told the workforce that they were now all in one chapel and that chapel bigotries and prejudices belonged to the past. My winding up went down well. I borrowed a phrase from a famous speech by Hugh Gaitskell, never a hero of mine. We did not guarantee success; only fools would do that and we were not fools. "But we do guarantee that we shall fight, and fight, and, having fought, we shall fight again." In retrospect the rhetoric sounds meaningless but it seemed relevant at the time.

A MEETING with the Prime Minister, Harold Wilson, was arranged for the Thursday afternoon. Jimmy Jack was to lead the delegation and it was to be held under the aegis of the STUC. There was some resistance to our attendance from Jack. "I don't really want any of you lads to attend the meeting with the PM. You know he doesn't really talk with shop stewards," he told us at Glasgow Airport, shaking his head in disapproval. I argued that we were the experts, best qualified to tell Wilson of the situation. Jack glowered at me and shook his head. Now I was nearing boiling point.

Alex Kitson, then the national organiser of the Transport and General Workers' Union, who was accompanying Jack, drew him aside and then came back to suggest we could attend if we gave a commitment not to make a contribution. I accepted on these terms but privately decided that if asked to do so by the Prime Minister I could hardly decline to argue on behalf of the workforce in my own words.

At No 10 we were ushered into a large room with a leather-topped rectangular table. Willie Ross, then Secretary of State for Scotland, greeted us. I had canvassed for Ross before he first became MP for Kilmarnock, my home town, and we had kept up our friendship over the 28 years or so since. He introduced me to Wilson as, "Allister, you know, Mrs Mackie's son from Kilmarnock."

Wilson gave me a puzzled look and then allowed his face to crease into a friendly grin. "Of course, that small woman from Kilmarnock. I remember her well."

We got down to business. Jack presented our case brilliantly – the need for industry in the West of Scotland, the flight of skilled labour from the area, the need for a Scottish-based newspaper. Bill (Sir William) Gray, then Lord Provost of Glasgow, followed up, stressing the needs of the city. Kitson was left with little to add. Wilson listened intently, asking the occasional question. He filled his pipe and as he puffed it he peered at me through the smoke.

"Now, Allister, tell me your version of what has happened and what ought to be done to save the situation." I was caught off guard with his question but lost no time in putting the argument on behalf of the workforce. Burke and Macgee, fellow delegates from the committee, backed me up. Wilson wound up nicely with a promise to make an approach to Beaverbrook to continue with the Glasgow operation. We were gracefully ushered to the door and within seconds were back in the street again. In Albion Street that evening we made our reports to the Action Committee. All came to the same conclusion. If our jobs were to be saved we would have to do it ourselves. We formally agreed to form a co-operative. We did it for differing reasons. Some thought that all sorts of people would come running to help. To me they were simplistic. McNamara and I had discussed it at length and I remember his argument clearly. It had to be done as a protest against unemployment. If we did manage to get the paper off the ground it had to be correct politically. We must not let some of the journalists, with their Beaverbrook breeding, determine its political outlook. And if they did succeed in the end of the day, we must have the courage to destroy the paper even though we ourselves had created it. But the argument seemed no more than academic. How could a group of unemployed tradesmen create a newspaper? It had never been even attempted before.

Next morning I flew the kite on BBC radio's *Good Morning Scotland*. I admitted that we were seriously considering a co-operative and stood back to await the reaction. It was instant. A publican from Bo'ness, Charlie Auld, that night phoned me at Albion Street to make the first commitment to invest £100. On the same evening William Wolfe presented himself to the Action Committee. At that time he was the chairman of the Scottish National Party and a near neighbour of mine in Bathgate. I scarcely knew him at the time and, being a member of the Labour Party myself, had misgivings about his concern. There seemed a danger that he would use our struggle to gain some form of ready-made publicity for himself or his party. Ever since his first introduction I have regretted my misgivings. It was never the case.

Within 48 hours he had examined the books of the company that were made available to him by a very disenchanted general manager, prepared a feasibility analysis of our intentions and declared that, given the assumption of reasonable advertising content and a circulation of around 200,000, the paper could survive. This was all we needed. The

Express circulation in Scotland was then over 550,000. Surely we could capture at least half of those readers. A hastily convened meeting of the workforce held the following day endorsed the committee's proposal for a co-operative and agreed to continue with the production of the paper to allow the committee to start negotiations.

The mass meeting showed an exciting enthusiasm. For most, hope had died instantly but now the workforce committed itself to investing a proportion of its redundancy money, leaving it to the committee to decide how much would be required from each. The first six days of our death sentence had been served.

CHAPTER TWO

What's in a name?

NO NEWSPAPER ever dies quietly. For the *Scottish Daily Express* it was a gigantic wake. Men who had given a lifetime of sober service underwent an instant transformation worthy of Jekyll and Hyde. Within hours, habitual optimists disintegrated into inconsolable pessimists. Social drinkers matched seasoned bar-flies glass-for-glass.

Closeted in the cleaners' room on the sixth floor, the Action Committee, by now 12 in number, denied themselves the solace of drink. We were far removed from the cauldron of erupting emotions below. In the tiny, smoke-polluted room, the committee were setting out on what would prove to be the strangest, the most exciting, the most fantastic odyssey of their lives. Not all would finish the journey but those who did would never be quite the same again. That was ahead; for now we saw ourselves as trade unionists, moderate and reasonable. McNamara and I were the only known political activists but the general sympathy was to the Left. Like Malvolio, most felt greatness had been thrust upon them; again like Malvolio, many of us felt slightly ridiculous. But we could not just walk away and leave our comrades leaderless in the shadow of the dole queue.

There was a hotch-potch of views in those early days. Some of the journalists wanted to form their own co-operative and have the paper printed under contract. Others were making statements to their colleagues on other newspapers which did not match the official attitudes of the Action Committee. They had to be disciplined. There was a move to pull the caseroom out of the struggle for God only knows what reason; but it failed. The general secretaries went through the motions of inviting Rupert Murdoch of the *Sun* and Sir Hugh Fraser of *The Glasgow Herald* to take over the printing of the paper –

Sir Hugh had already bought the *Citizen* title for £1.7m. But we ignored these digressions and they proved to be little more.

I phoned Jocelyn Stevens in the Fleet Street office of the *Express* to tell him of our plans to launch our own newspaper and asked to be considered for a first option on the building. He told me the price of the property was £2.4m and that we could have the first option for a three-month period. I wasn't too surprised with his reply. This actually was the response I had expected. Public reaction to the closure of the plant had been extremely critical and Beaverbrook needed to ingratiate themselves with the public. On March 28, only nine days after he had given us official notice to quit, Stevens gave us official written confirmation that we had the first option on the building.

But within 24 hours we had lost it again. On the evening of March 29 we asked Ian Brodie, the editor of the *Scottish Daily Express,* to insert a statement from the Action Committee on the front page. Brodie refused but agreed to insert it somewhere in an inside page. Now the statement, prepared by Macgee and Nathan Goldberg, another journalist who had joined the committee, was really quite innocuous. It merely stated that the workforce regretted the closure of the Glasgow office and that the committee pledged that it would return with its own paper before long from the ashes of the *Scottish Daily Express*. Brodie could have made a story of the statement on the front page without losing any blood but he refused point blank. Equally it must be admitted that the statement would have been every bit as significant on an inside page as far as we were concerned. However, our reaction was to have the story set in type, then to seize the front page as it was about to leave the caseroom and insert the story. Other departments were waiting to handle the paper but at the last moment the management called off the transport. Only a few papers were printed and circulated. Stevens, because of our action, took away our first option on the building but restored it again on the Sunday after the rumpus had died down. I thought a lot about that little escapade on my drive back home to Bathgate that night. It had been rather a pointless exercise. All our effort had achieved nothing. Unless we changed our entire outlook we would be continually engaged in those silly little expressions of protest and the time for protest was over. We were now forming a co-operative to start our own business. What good would our trade union reflexes do us in future? None, as far as I could see. We were no longer on the defensive; we had to attack for once – not a wild cavalry charge against the forces of the establishment but a carefully planned attack on its principles. Could the committee change its attitudes and escape from its traditional confrontation, or were they prisoners of their prejudices? One of the unpalatable priorities we would have to recognise was the need to establish a friendly relationship with Beaverbrook.

March 3

TO INVOLVE the workforce in the struggle we had arranged for the occupation of the building. It was a bit of a cheat, really. Stevens in London, when I told him of our plans, spiked my guns by agreeing that it was a good idea. He then proceeded to supply us with telephones, accommodation and the use of the canteen. It was no problem for Beaverbrook at that time since there were a good many of the journalists still working on the premises alongside copy typists, telephonists and wire-room personnel. But the workforce seemed happy to feel involved in the struggle and that was important.

The first essential on the Sunday after the closure was to move from our cramped headquarters on the sixth floor to more comfortable accommodation on the fourth. Previously it had been the advertising department, and so it was well served with phones. Within a couple of days an established working pattern was emerging. We no longer sweated our days out from early morning to near midnight. Almost for the first time for many of us we were working a regular nine-to-five routine.

It was not until this period that I had a chance to take stock of a hectic fortnight. For the first time in my life I had made a TV appearance. That in itself was an experience. Not until the first time at the STV studio did it occur to me that the fine sun-tans and ruddy complexions were mainly the result of concoctions from bottles applied by deft make-up girls. The problem was to remember to take the make-up off afterwards. Once I was halfway to Bathgate before I remembered to clean my face. I shudder yet to think what the reception might have been at my destination, the Miners' Welfare Club.

Occasionally at that time I would try to make an assessment of my personal position. I felt a deepening resentment. The newspaper world had been good to me. Wages had been reasonable and I had enjoyed the life. At that time my marriage was only six months old; I had just taken out a mortgage, for the first time in my life, for a house. I was living in a town I had scarcely heard of until two years before and was still trying to establish my identity there. For the first time in my life I had more than £3000 in my bank book – all put there by Beaverbrook redundancy payments, wages in lieu of notice, pension refunds and other bits and pieces. And so I thought of starting from the beginning again. Perhaps I'd invest the lot in a public house and start a new career in the licensed trade. Few other prospects then appealed to me.

But here I was, tied up in a piece of trade union protest that I believed would take us nowhere. It could well cost me all of my little nest-egg. And it seemed such a crazy dream, to run our own newspaper. No-one had ever done it before or, I suspected, even attempted it. Ken Bryson of the BBC, a former *Express* colleague, was very difficult in his interviews with me. But I liked his style because, as I soon learned, the hostile interview gave me more scope to put over the points I wanted to project. In one of our earlier interviews he asked me if I were not indulging in a pipe-dream. In my reply I recalled George Bernard Shaw's Father Keegan, who argued: "A dream is a reality in the womb of time." It was necessary, I reminded him, to dream before you could create. I was never again accused of being too idealistic but within myself I believed myself to be so.

THE SIT-IN began but at no time was it a great success. Throughout the building, at any one time, you would have been lucky to count more than 70 heads. The fault was perhaps my own. I asked the chapels to organise themselves into rotas so that there would be 24-hour coverage but said that the Action Committee did not want any heroic exhibitions, that the sit-in was a token one and required no great sacrifices. My advice was taken too literally in most departments. But there was sufficient coverage to claim honestly that the sit-in was taking place. Months later I learned that compared with many other similar industrial actions, ours was relatively successful.

It became an early priority to name the paper. It would serve as a rallying point for our workforce, a slogan. Various names were looked at. Bert Liddell, the treasurer, wanted to call it the *Phoenix* because it would have risen from the ashes of the old *Express*. It wasn't a popular suggestion. The *Daily Scot* sounded too much like a railway train. The *Independent Scot* evoked the SNP. And so it went on. By this time, with the help of a sympathetic lawyer, we had formed ourselves into a company called the Employees Enterprise, so what about the *Daily Enterprise*? It didn't sound right either.

The issue was soon resolved. Editorial artists Albert Tonner and Bill Young had been asked to produce two dummies, one a broadsheet and the other a tabloid. Macgee, approached by them for a title, said: "Just put down anything at all in the meantime." Tonner, once he had finished his dummy, couldn't leave a blank space at the top of the paper and so inserted the most obvious title – the *Scottish Daily News*. In the absence of any alternative, it was accepted unanimously. The previous *Daily News*, as far as we were aware, had been started by Dickens in the nineteenth century. Perhaps it was time for another.

Despite all the publicity we were receiving we were really making no headway. We were treated more like freaks than serious people who intended to launch their own newspaper. There was public curiosity, but whether it could be transformed into interest and involvement had to be discovered. The fault was not ours alone. No amount of conviction or determination could supply the business knowledge we desperately needed. It would have to be found . . . but from where?

Tirelessly, to create public involvement, John Ferguson made arrangements for a meeting of leading figures in the West of Scotland. Lord Provost Gray made the Glasgow City Chambers available and agreed to chair it.

April 10

THE TURN-OUT was good, very good. There were representatives from industry, banking, commerce, the universities, the political parties, religious organisations and the trade unions. There was a hardly a facet of our complex society that was not represented that day.

Gray opened the meeting with a sympathetic appeal for help for us and then asked me to speak on behalf of the committee. First I put the case for the need to preserve as many skills as possible in the West of Scotland. Secondly, there was a crying need to do whatever we could to preserve our national culture and way of life. The bulk of papers read in Scotland were either printed or owned in England. It was a time for beating the Scottish drum.

The response was tremendous. The audience rose to my appeal for involvement with an earnestness that was mildly disturbing. Perhaps the idea wasn't so crazy after all. If those people could look at our ideas with enthusiasm, then just perhaps . . .

Tom Band, representing the Department of Trade and Industry, was on his feet proposing a feasibility study by Strathclyde University (as Hugh Brown had already suggested). His department might be willing to pay for half its cost if the City of Glasgow would cough up the other half. He looked over at Gray questioningly.

Gray fidgeted, then nodded his head slowly. "I believe that our council can be persuaded . . . I cannot say for sure, of course . . . Yes, I'm sure it will be all right."

We no longer stood alone. It had been a good meeting.

WITHIN 48 hours a team of management consultants had arrived from Chesters College, the Strathclyde University business school. It was headed by Allan Gay. He came, I believe, a sceptic. But within a few days he was developing a keener enthusiasm. His first concern was our proposed staffing levels. "Oh, around six or seven hundred," was my unacademic reply to his inquiry. His grey blue eyes, through rimless glasses, gave me a piercing look. "Are you telling me that you haven't yet worked out the number of people that will be employed on the paper?" I replied: "We are determined that we shall employ as many as we can. We have a problem of unemployment in our trade . . ."

I tailed off uncertainly. He shook his head sadly. "No, Allister, you've got it all wrong. You must pare down the staff to an absolute minimum, make the enterprise as profit-worthy as possible, grudge every penny you have to spend, and generally be as mean as possible. It's perhaps a difficult lesson for you to learn as a trade unionist but if you don't there's no chance of your succeeding. You might as well pack up and not waste any more of your time and money."

With more than a thousand unemployed friends breathing down my neck, I could not absorb his advice. Nor could anyone else on the committee with the possible exception of Jimmy Russell, a financial journalist and old friend who had by this time been enlisted. It was not possible to think in terms of employing as few people as possible when there were so many out of work. Surely this could not be the answer to our plight? We felt a terrible unease and were beginning to wonder if he was really as sympathetic as we had at first believed.

But within two weeks I had turned round completely and was attempting to cut our staffing levels to about 500. Gay's message eventually had to be heeded. What we had to do was to think in terms of creating jobs. There were no jobs to be saved: they had all already been lost. We would have to create something viable which would create jobs and viability would have to take precedence over many other considerations. That lesson was still to be absorbed as we slowly tried to unlearn all the attitudes and emotions that had stood us in good stead as trade unionists. They were now beginning to threaten our continued existence.

THE PRESSURE was beginning to get to us. Nathan Goldberg, conscripted for his ability to think on his feet, spoke of a particular worry at that time. A reliable journalist friend had told him that the Special Branch were watching us and had photographed one of the mass meetings outside the building from a small green van parked nearby in College Street, and that our private phones were being tapped. "It's really a bit of a giggle," said Goldberg, "but it shouldn't be allowed to go on." He added that his friend's source was a senior police officer in the city.

I looked round the table at a circle of friends. It would have been hard to imagine a less likely collection of revolutionaries. The numbers had by now crawled up to 17, and I classed none as dangerous to the security of the country. And yet I believed Goldberg. So too did McNamara, who declared that it was the Establishment's way of defending itself. "They don't know what we are, but in some strange, obscure way, we make them feel insecure. Therefore we are their enemies. But we should do nothing about it. They can do us no harm with their silly little games."

His advice was taken, yet we were all convinced that the bugging was happening. You could discern a distinct click-click when phoning out, with a loss in quality. We had nothing to hide, so why kick up a fuss?

CHAPTER THREE

Ce n'est pas la guerre

IT WAS now time to press the Government into making a statement of support. A meeting was arranged with a junior Minister at the Department of Industry, Eric Deakin. It was held in the Department's offices in Victoria Street, just next to the Houses of Parliament. Goldberg, David Grant a process engraver, and I made up the delegation. Before we went in I warned the others that the meeting might not be all that pleasant but that we were not in the business of being friendly. We were looking for help, not sympathy.

Government Ministers, I was soon to learn, seem to inhabit the centre of an onion: no matter how many layers are peeled off there is yet another to be tackled. He is protected by protocol and the formal theatre of the meeting. He appears personally; he is in obvious command; he has immediate access to facts and statutes; and then there is the civil service, his bodyguard and shield. But if the appellant is sufficiently determined, and if he has some empathy with the Minister, he may eventually find the human being at the core.

Deakin smiled urbanely. He was charming, well-groomed, long-haired and dressed in the modern manner as befitted an up-and-coming politician then in his mid-thirties (he later disappeared into obscurity).

"Well, of course we should like to help you, be assured of that. Nothing would give us greater pleasure. We have nothing but the utmost admiration for what you lads are attempting. It is exciting and terribly ambitious, but I'm afraid that it may prove difficult for the Government to give you the help you are looking for although, of course, I am not in a position to speak on behalf of the Government."

He went on at some length, saying neither yea nor nay. This

ability seems to be a pre-requisite for all politicians. I was just about to switch off my mental concentration, a weakness of mine when there seems nothing worthwhile to listen to, when I heard him say: ". . . so really, you see, initially the business community of Scotland ought to give you the help you seek. When they have given a commitment of support, and I must stress that the commitment will have to be absolute, then, but not until then, will the Government be in a position to give you a definite answer . . ."

That was all I needed to cut short his flow. "Mr Deakin, I have heard more than I feared I might hear. All my life I have worked for a Labour Government, for 28 years now. I did so because I believe that we all must together fight for the creation of a socialist society. I make no definitions between left and right wing; these are journalists' accommodations. I accept that if one is in the Labour Party then one is by that fact a socialist?"

He nodded his head in agreement.

"Good. Then let me tell you that your arguments are far worse than I would have expected from Enoch Powell. How are the businessmen in Scotland going to give us help until the Government makes clear its own involvement? And anyway do you seriously believe that they will contribute towards a workers' co-operative that will be producing a newspaper obviously slanted to supporting Labour? It is your responsibility, the Government's, to support us and to create employment, not the business world's. Your argument astonishes me. It is neither intelligent nor socialist. And you have a responsibility to the Labour Movement to carry out socialist policies, and for socialist reasons. That is why I and thousands like me worked for your return. Now you must face up to the responsibilities of being an elected socialist or get out and let someone else do the job in your stead."

The senior of his advisers then interrupted my flow.

"Really, Mr Mackie, you have no right to . . ."

"Sir, you have no right to interrupt my meeting with the Minister unless by invitation and I didn't invite you to. If I had wanted a meeting with your good self I would have asked for one. I am speaking to the Minister."

He blinked his eyes in disbelief, as though I had appeared from another planet. I swung my chair back round to face Deakin and continued my tirade. And that was the fatal error. Its four legs collapsed under my weight and I fell in a heap among them with my indignation and dignity in tatters. Deakin looked appalled. His obvious concern, the tension of the meeting, were suddenly irresistibly funny, an enormous joke. It took me at least a couple of minutes before I could control my laughter and resume in a secure and tested seat. The incident was rounded off by my asking Deakin if the chair were specially designed for disposing of awkward customers.

But I had done all that I had set out to do. The Minister now knew there was going to be a fight and with the possibility it could be a dirty one. I pointed out that if the Government refused to help they might regret the political implications of their decision. At that time Labour was a minority party in Government, another election was imminent. If help were not seen to be forthcoming the Scottish Nats would use the situation to attack the Labour Party. It would not be inconceivable for them to win another 20 seats from Labour. Every step would have to be taken to prevent this happening. As I spoke, Deakin showed a new and more intense interest in what I was saying. This was language he understood and appreciated. This was the world of party politics and as such was infinitely more interesting than his departmental responsibilities. After another 20 minutes of question and discussion we were finished.

Outside Goldberg shook his head. "At first I thought you were being a bit hard on him. He's a good lad and we don't want to lose our friends. But it turned out all right in the end."

"Nat, our friends are those who help us. The others are enemies and bad ones, no matter how sympathetic they appear to be."

WE DID not simply sit around and wait for the Chesters team to report. We would need finance from sources other than the Government, help from institutions, unions and individuals. Almost every prominent British businessman believed to have radical or socialist leanings was contacted. Among them was Robert Maxwell of Headington Hall, Oxford. He was a former Labour MP and a successful businessman, even if there had been a time when his credibility had been challenged by the Department of Trade. We then arranged a meeting in Glasgow exclusively for business and financial interests. Ferguson, again left with the task of making the contacts, phoned Maxwell, among others. To his delight Maxwell claimed a genuine interest. It was a change in a monotonous day of bland refusals.

At that time Armstrong and Goldberg were in London doing the rounds of tycoons, with little luck. They were told of Maxwell's interest. On the spur of the moment Goldberg suggested phoning him and he agreed to meet them at his London house. The two, slightly bewildered, left their dingy hotel room and arrived at his house in Montpelier Square feeling some apprehension. An Indonesian servant opened the door for them and ushered them into a ground floor room. They were brought a pot of tea. While drinking it they were joined by a smartly dressed West Indian, in pin stripes and with a rolled umbrella. He did not introduce himself but joined them in tea. When all three were ushered into the presence of Maxwell in his office on the floor above, the West Indian identified himself as Maxwell's legal adviser who had been particularly invited to be present. Maxwell first inquired about cash for the campaign and the cost of the trip to London. He was told by Armstrong that despite help for the Fighting Fund from unions and the public, it was a hard struggle.

From his jacket Maxwell produced a wad of notes and threw them on Armstrong's knee. "How much is there?" he asked.

Armstrong counted them. "Eighty quid."

A further fumbling in other pockets produced another wad of notes and the manicured fingers peeled off a £20 note. "That should make it one hundred pounds, eh?"

Within the next hour Goldberg and Armstrong were to learn quite a bit about the use of telephones and how to make business contacts. Maxwell's charm seemed as cultivated as his accent. Everything about him seemed big, vital, alive. In particular they noticed his eyes. He seldom seemed to turn his head as he looked around him, letting his eyes do the turning for him. They were like a lizard's eyes as they darted around. At machine-gun speed he made a series of phone calls, meanwhile insisting that the committee must as a first priority engage a top management team. He possibly had just the man for the *News*.

Then he announced: "To show my support for your struggle I commit myself to investing 50p for every pound that you yourselves invest. What do you think about that?"

But before they could muster a reply the phone calls started again. Jocelyn Stevens was contacted in London and Sir Hugh Fraser in Glasgow. In his call to Fraser, he upset Armstrong and Goldberg by referring to the Action Committee as a group of well-meaning "boy scouts" who knew nothing about what they were attempting to do. In retrospect the comment, though cruel, had a basis of justification.

Armstrong and Goldberg sat in silence throughout the entire performance. When another cup of tea was delivered, Armstrong noticed that Maxwell's cup, although belonging to the same set as the others, was in actual fact larger. The whole setting, the phone calls, the name-dropping, the presence of a lawyer who played no part in the meeting, the rapid questioning, the larger-sized cup – what did they signify? It was impossible to be sure. But on the way back to Glasgow, Armstrong and Goldberg agreed that Maxwell was the first indication that there might be cash available, if the workers played their cards right.

AS THEY were heading home, Richard Briston, professor of accountancy at Strathclyde University, came as Maxwell's representative to the meeting of financiers arranged by the committee. I wish I could forget that meeting. We tried to talk a sackful of generalities when the financiers were asking hard, searching questions. What sort of shares do you intend to issue? Will there be an issue of equities? Do you anticipate a cash-flow problem within the first three months? Will your company be structured under the provisions of the Companies Act? And many more questions that not only could I not answer, but did not even begin to understand. As the meeting tortured itself to a close I mentally dismissed it as an absolute disaster. It had exposed us to ourselves as ignoramuses who knew nothing of the world we hoped soon to populate.

As the meeting was breaking up and the invited audience was inevitably dismissing us as ten-day freaks, I was approached by Briston, a man in his mid-thirties, slightly balding, on the heavy side. He introduced himself in a quiet, Norfolk voice and somewhat surprised me by asking to be taken back to Albion Street. On the way he told me in confidence that he was sending a report to Maxwell and added: "You have an awful lot to learn in company structure and finance before you can hope to make any headway. You were obviously well out of your depth today. Today's questions were deliberately framed to discredit you."

Within an hour Briston was addressing the committee. He advised us of the need to organise ourselves and to draw up a company structure. He offered his personal help and that of a firm of accountants of which he was an associate. He also advised us to engage a firm of solicitors which would have a greater degree of public acceptability than our existing advisers.

The dream was actually beginning to take shape, slowly. Briston was a lifeline for us. He wasn't encumbered by our trade union attitudes; he was capable of taking an objective look at problems and thinking outwith the history of our involvement with Beaverbrook. We, as a committee, had still to reach that stage. But the important thing was that he actually believed our dream was attainable.

New problems were being created daily. The editorial planning board, which was preparing the content and design of the new paper, was becoming a major headache. Its members were setting themselves above the rest of the workforce and the Action Committee, for which they had a growing and obvious contempt. They would have to be confronted sooner rather than later.

Soon Briston was becoming a regular visitor to the committee meetings. One day he made a proposal which revealed a growing divide within our committee. Little suspecting, he casually and innocently proposed that we consider a change of name for the company. I quickly glanced over at Blyth, sensing that he would be the first to object. His suspicions of Briston were manifesting themselves daily. Blyth had opposed the change of lawyers because, irrespective of their professional standing, our original advisers had stood by us. Now, with brows furrowed in a scowl of mistrust, he resisted the change of name. He argued that we were an employees' enterprise, were proud of that fact, and should let the whole world know it. Russell countered by saying that as long as the company's principles were unchanged, the name was immaterial. But in Blyth's attitude I discerned a challenge to my own position. Earlier, I had argued the need to reappraise our trade union thinking. Our struggle required weapons more sophisticated than the cudgel or the slogans of militancy. As the debate raged on, I could detect the widening gap between those trade unionists who were capable of change and the troglodytes, as I called them, who were not. Nevertheless, Briston's proposal was at last taken up and after a few days there emerged the name *Scottish News Enterprises Ltd.*

May 4

THE SKY was overcast as Russell, Armstrong, Briston and I left Glasgow Airport for our arranged meeting with Robert Maxwell in Oxford. Somewhere over the Lake District Briston began to tell us of our host for the day, his personality, his background in commerce and a rough assessment of his capital. He concluded with the words, "But you must judge him on your own assessments of him. I have no wish to influence you."

At the time the words seeped their way into my consciousness like a warning, but I didn't pursue the thought any further. It was enough to be going to meet someone who professed an interest in our struggle and seemed prepared to follow up with cash. The arrangements were that we were to be met at Heathrow by Maxwell's chauffeur and his red Rolls-Royce. Armstrong joked about using the car-phone to ring up his drinking cronies in his usual haunt on Saturday afternoons. "The lads up in the Calton would be knocked cold if I rang up The Treble Two (a public house) from a chauffeur-driven Rolls-Royce in the south of England."

The dream did not come true. At Heathrow there was no-one to meet us. No message had been left. Briston phoned Oxford and then, full of apologies, told us that Maxwell was there all right but that we would have to find our own way there. No apologies or explanations came from Maxwell. In heavy rain, Briston drove us down in a hired car and on the way said: "I ought to have warned you that this might have happened. I should have known better by this time than to have expected him to be there."

Headington Hall stands on the south side of the university city, well off the road, and is approached by a tree-lined ramped road dotted with signs declaring it private. Maxwell was there to greet us, hand outstretched and welcoming. He was a paragon of charm and courtesy. In the lounge to which we had been ushered I noted the furniture – a baby grand piano, beside it a harp; antique furniture, a chess set in jade.

Through the french windows I could see the rain splattering down on to a swimming pool in the garden grounds. It was, I thought, like the setting of an Agatha Christie novel and half expected to glimpse Hercule Poirot. Instead we were introduced to Mike Cudlipp, then of *London Broadcasting,* and a well-known Fleet Street journalist from a famous stable.

We soon got down to business round an oblong table covered with green baize, Maxwell at its head. He embraced us with a dart of his eyes. "Now to start with, men," he said, "you must ensure that you do not get caught up in a dichotomy . . ."

He paused, raised his bushy eyebrows. Then, pointing his face in turn at each of us, excluding Briston, he added: "You all know, of course, just exactly what a dichotomy is . . .?"

None of us responded but he went on with his explanation anyway. "Well, this is most important, so listen closely to what I'm about to tell you." Having made sure that we would at all costs avoid a dichotomy, he proceeded with the real business of the meeting.

"You gentlemen, I believe, have a formula that all industry must adopt if it is to survive. The involvement of workers in the running of their own industries is crucial. As an indication of my support I am committing myself to investing 50p to every £1 that your members invest. Now what do you think of that?"

"You realise, of course, that our lads have committed themselves to raising £300,000?"

Maxwell looked at me with a pained expression and, with palms turned upwards in a mannerism that we would all learn to recognise before long, continued: "So then I am committed already to £150,000."

Armstrong, sceptical as always, pushed back the bridge of his spectacles with his right middle finger, then pointed his fore-finger in the direction of Maxwell. "Tell us what's in it for you. No-one in his right mind is going to make a commitment like that unless there's a return somewhere along the line."

The publisher's eyes flashed round all of us as we waited for his answer. We were watching him intently.

"What's in it for me?" he repeated. "Political capital."

Russell introduced himself by clearing his throat. "You mean that you will receive publicity by your involvement with us that can be converted into political credibility?"

After a short pause Maxwell, no longer smiling and thinking deeply, slowly nodded his head. "Yes, that's exactly what I mean."

It made sense to us. To a man like Maxwell, political capital was essential. He had been beaten in the General Election a few months before and it was guaranteed that there would be another election before the year was out.

Mike Cudlipp was not there by chance. As a further proof of Maxwell's stated good intentions, he now commissioned Cudlipp to go to Glasgow, live with us, advise us, guide us and help us in any way that was necessary. He would be maintained by Maxwell and officially employed by him as a consultant.

Business over, we were served with drinks before going for a meal, where we were entertained by Maxwell's charming wife. But Maxwell was the ultimate charmer. His speech, considering it was not his mother tongue, was impeccable. His natural power and vitality were impressive, energising those around him. It could prove a great help to the struggle if it could be harnessed properly. But could we hope to control him?

As we drove back to London, Briston seemed to sense my fears. He said: "Watch him closely." He then recalled the affair of Maxwell, Pergamon and the Board of Trade. It brought our feet back to the ground.

FOUR DAYS later, true to Maxwell's promises, Mike Cudlipp took up residence in the Albany Hotel in Glasgow. Within a week Cudlipp and Briston together had transformed the workforce from woolly-headed but determined hopefuls into an army with a clear objective. With his endless energy and enthusiasm Cudlipp prodded us into making only relevant decisions and lent a managerial outlook that was essential for our continuance as a viable force. It is impossible for me to give an accurate assessment of his own feelings but I suspect he joined us an absolute sceptic. Little wonder, for there was little cause for optimism. The journalists were by this time proving themselves a daily problem with their open display of suspicion, contempt and hostility towards the Action Committee. What good could possibly come out of the rabble that we were?

Yet another and more fundamental problem was the growing in-fighting within the Action Committee. Blyth emerged as spokesman for the dissidents, who included almost half the committee in the early stages. Their hostility boiled down to their inability to change their attitudes in a changing situation. They were still fighting Beaverbrook. Armstrong, to my deep disappointment, joined ranks with Blyth, and it was many weeks before he was capable of changing; from that point he made a remarkable contribution. There were, of course, a hard core who never really deviated from their support of me and my style of leadership – Russell, McNamara, Crossan, Hooper. But their support was never for myself personally. They accepted the need for a change of attitudes, and were capable of that change. Although we seldom discussed business out with the actual meetings, we seldom voted other than as a group. Macgee used to phone me at home and advise me to pick my friends more carefully, but his playing footsy with both camps put him outwith my circle of trust.

Yet I never lost control of the committee. This I did by the expedient of not allowing a vote to take place until I was happy about the outcome. There were always enough members in the middle ground to assure me of a reasonable majority. It wasn't necessarily democratic, but all we needed to destroy us was one or two bad decisions, no more. And I couldn't run that risk.

Cudlipp's arrival was a great relief to me. Within days he was tackling our staffing levels and going into our proposed management structures in depth. In the background the management consultants from Strathclyde were still beavering away and in time became very interested in our ideas for a company structure. They came up with a proposal that there should be a two-tier structure. It was a pretty complicated hotchpotch of ideas and seemed to me to be something dreamed up by somebody playing at a game. It had no relation to the reality we were living in. Their proposals invested all the real authority in the hands of a management team, with the workforce playing an advisory role. It was not my concept of a co-operative in any sense. The consultants did not seem capable of looking on the management team as just another, though essential, group of workers. And they still held the prejudice that ordinary workers were incapable of making executive decisions. That function, therefore, had to be left exclusively to the management team.

We naturally insisted that the workforce should have its representation with executive control, otherwise we could not have escaped from the confrontation trap that all industry is held in. When we insisted on our concept of workforce representatives having executive control, Gay and his team retaliated with the comment that no industry could be run by an endless procession of committee meetings. Their comments hurt me more than anything else did at the time. It was an unintended insult to us, thus all the more hurtful. To be fair, their attitudes may well have been conditioned by our behaviour as a committee. If so then their comments were understandable; but they were still wrong. From the time we discarded their ideas of the company structure the Strathclyde team seemed less enthusiastic about our chances of survival.

Those were exciting days when Cudlipp first arrived. The committee's first impressions of him soon gave way to feelings of respect and affection as we learned to live with him and his ways and he with ours. But within 48 hours his arrival was almost forgotten with the weight of our own problems. It was on the following Friday evening. My wife and I took the chance to relax by having a night out at a dinner-dance at the Masonic Arms in Armadale in West Lothian, not far from my home town of Bathgate. It wasn't a stunning success by any means: my head was full of the problems of Albion Street. Jocelyn Stevens was by this time pressurising us to clear out of the building, with veiled threats of taking legal action against some members of the Action Committee. Hooper and Ferguson were on duty in the building watching for signs of hardening Beaverbrook attitudes. At around 10pm there seemed to be a build-up of activity, with outside contractors buzzing around inspecting the machinery – and that on a Friday night! Hooper phoned me with his report as arranged at Armadale to let me know what was happening. He felt they were beginning to show their hand. "John and I are both certain that they're going to take some of the machinery out."

I doubted his interpretation. Beaverbrook didn't need to act in an underhand way. They held almost all the trump cards. Our only assets were our mounting public support and our self-belief. But Hooper, Ferguson and many of the others in the Action Committee were beginning to feel the need to step up the aggro; the progress we were making was good, encouraging, but not enough to satisfy the red corpuscles. Perhaps it is necessary at times to recognise the need for the dramatic. "Phone up every member of the committee and bring them in immediately. Tell them to bring in bedding and food and be in the building by midnight." It was then 10.55pm.

My social evening came to an abrupt halt when I rejoined the company to tell my wife of the latest development. On the way home to Bathgate to pick up my rations and bedding I thought about the developing situation. Inevitably personal relations would be strained. Our entente with Beaverbook would suffer. Worst of all we were concentrating less on preparing for the production of a new newspaper and more on fighting our previous employers. It was doubtful if the decision were correct but it was emotional, spectacular and in the best of trade union traditions. I remembered the comment of the French cavalry marshal when he witnessed the Charge of the Light Brigade: "*C'est magnifique, mais ce n'est pas la guerre.*"

WITHIN 40 minutes I had arrived at Albion Street. Bob French, the security chief, welcomed me with a friendly nod of the head. "There's nothing happening that I know of. And if there was something about to happen, they would have let me know of it first."

On the fourth floor there was rising excitement among the committee members. A meeting was soon convened which endorsed my decision to call the members in. The sleep-in was on. Crossan was appointed the rations convener and head cook. He turned out to be an inspired choice. We also passed a rule that every member would take a half-hour walk every morning irrespective of the weather. The constitutionals were carefully scheduled to ensure a maximum occupation at any one time. Then it was time, around 2.30am, for bedding down. It was warm for the season and sleep did not come easily. My own little patch where I laid down my borrowed air-bed was at the telegirls' supervisor's desk. It was by the window and what little breath of air that blew was mine. It was soon being joked about as the executive suite.

On the first night I went over in my crowded head the events of the past six weeks. Already it seemed a lifetime. I longed for some order in my life, something I could rely on, something that for better or worse I could say was my lot. During my days in the RAF I had felt exactly the same longing. It would hit me most heading south in a train after a few days' leave. As you left Edinburgh Waverley there was a tenement block on the right. All the lights seemed to be on and if the train was moving slowly you could steal a glimpse of the private lives being lived there. They weren't exactly happy lives, no doubt, because it would be easy to let misery dominate your world in a run-down tenement block. But they seemed reasonably settled and secure and that was all that I believed I needed to create my world of happiness. In the Services I had felt rootless, unsettled, with no base to build my life on. Here I was again, unemployed with a blank wall staring me in the face. It was absolutely crazy to think of raising three-and-a-half million pounds, the total amount required, yet we had to make the effort. And even if we could raise the cash would our journalists turn out a good newspaper? McNamara came back to this point time and again. He didn't trust their politics or their competence. But we couldn't walk away until we had tried, at least.

Soon, under advice and guidance from Briston and Cudlipp, we were gradually maturing a more professional outlook. Boyds, the Glasgow firm of solicitors, were now engaged as our legal advisers, and that single move was one of the most beneficial fundamental decisions that we made. They were a reservoir of strength and stability with their canny advice and dedication. Brian Dorman and Roy Patrick sweated blood for our enterprise, with an involvement far exceeding their professional obligations. I have never really fully understood the reasons for Boyds' involvement. It was never a question of financial gain to them since from the beginning there seemed little chance of their ever recovering their full fees. Nor can I believe that they felt a political commitment to support a co-operative. Yet their involvement was total and personal. Perhaps Gavin Boyd, the senior partner, simply felt he had a contribution to make to history. Whatever the reason we could never have survived without their support.

One of our earliest problems with the lawyers was that of creating a company structure that would meet the needs and vision of our co-operative. They had no precedents to guide them and had to construct the skeleton of our eventual organisation out of the vague, yet emphatic, principles we ourselves had laid down. The company would be controlled by the workforce, only the workforce, and could never be taken over by outside shareholders. We would stand or fall on those stated principles and if investors did not find them attractive then they would not invest. Eventually they came up with the formula that seemed to ensure the control by the workforce and at the same time offered some form of security and involvement for the investors.

CHAPTER FOUR

An insult from Maxwell

May 15

MAXWELL DECIDED to bring his involvement with us out into the open. He asked us to convene a mass meeting of the workforce that he could address. Arrangements were made for the meeting to be held on May 15 in the basement of the building. I met him at the airport before bringing him back to meet the other members of the committee and on the way to Albion Street updated him on our progress. It looked promising. Briston's firm of chartered accountants, French and Cowan, were preparing a feasibility study of our proposals and the workforce had conclusively committed themselves to investing the £300,000. Mike Cudlipp was doing a staffing assessment, especially on the editorial side. Whereas the Beaverbrook staffing requirements were over 300, we reduced the total number to ninety. This figure was more easily justified when we learned that this was the same staffing level in that department in the *Irish Times*. Macgee's contribution was: "How can you measure genius?" There was much to boast about, but overshadowing all the budding optimism was the report being prepared by the Strathclyde team of management consultants. Word was percolating through that after all it could be a bad one. This we didn't mind too badly, as long as it was accurate and objective. And this was our worry. On the eve of its publication Allan Gay had sent for Riddell to ask him how to calculate the projected advertising revenue of a newspaper – and that constitutes around half its potential income! How authoritative would the report be, we wondered, when they could not calculate so significant an element?

To many of the committee this was their first sight of Maxwell, and he was impressive. Again he conjured up names and contacts beyond our reach; this left the innocent with the impression that all that was required to get the paper off the ground was to hand over to him control of the entire operation.

In the local Georgic Restaurant we discussed the mass meeting that had been called for that afternoon. We were three at lunch, but poor Miss Baddeley, his secretary, had little chance to take her meal, having to take down in shorthand a barrage of notes and drafts for letters. And then he really shook me.

"Allister, during your address to the mass meeting this is what you will say. Miss Baddeley, take down these notes for Mr Mackie's speech and have them typed out for him ready for three o'clock. Now let me see. Do you address the workforce as comrades or brothers?"

I looked at him, aghast. No-one had ever suggested helping me to make speeches. I preferred to let the occasion and mood of the audience shape my words. Shaking my head in silent disbelief I allowed Maxwell to dictate to Miss Baddeley, at the same time deciding it would be a waste of time anyway.

Another shock was waiting. Looking at me intensely, Maxwell asked: "What about the questions?"

"What questions?"

"Come now, Allister. The workforce will be there, the TV cameras will be there. We must plant questions among the audience so that we'll be shown in a good light to everyone. Now give me a list of trusted people who will be capable of asking their questions articulately; possibly the journalists would be better at this sort of thing than the others."

I felt is as if someone had just walked over my grave. I suggested he contact the journalists on the committee.

His preparation for the meeting was successful. In the glare of the TV lights he answered detailed questioning apparently extempore. Jacketless, and in a striped shirt and red tie, he stood with one leg on a chair, like a brigand chief in charge of his crew. At the end of the meeting someone struck up with a chorus of "For He's a Jolly Good Fellow". A few joined in, but not many.

May 17

MAXWELL'S VISIT coincided with the date for the publication of the feasibility study by the Chesters management experts. He felt, as we all did at that time, that publication of an unfavourable report would kill us off almost overnight and we were by this time convinced a pessimistic forecast was being prepared. It would have to be stopped. Lord Provost Gray, as chairman of the committee which had set up the study, was asked for a meeting to discuss its contents. It was arranged for that evening at almost midnight in the Lord Provost's ante-room. On the way over to it Maxwell acted the big fish in the small pond. "Just leave it to me. I know exactly what I'm doing. I'll show you how to sort out these people."

What was the point in arguing? Anyway, as I trundled along beside him, I thought it might well be quite an experience to watch the big boys at the negotiating table. As a trade unionist my tactics had always been the same. Build up personal credibility through being straightforward and honest; show management that when you made a threat you were prepared to carry it out; and be reasonable at all times, even if it meant that your argument weakened in the process. And it was a successful formula. Over the years I had lost few arguments.

The room was not fully lit as we entered. Allan Gay was there with the Lord Provost and we settled down to discuss the business at a small table topped with green leather. Gay and Gray sat opposite Maxwell and myself.

I hadn't met Gray often enough to form an opinion of him, apart from gaining a fair respect for his clear and logical thinking. Gay, on the other hand, was a person for whom I had grown to feel affection. He was a man possibly in his mid-fifties, balding. Like myself, he was seldom well-groomed. He wore rimless glasses and talked rapidly in a high-pitched voice. He was sincere. At first I found him a pain in the neck as he kept asking us difficult and at times hostile questions. But we had come to understand that he was only doing his job as he saw it.

The pleasantries over, Gray handed us a bound type-written report. He was obviously ill-at-ease, preferring not to meet my gaze until I had taken a look at the findings.

"I'm afraid it's not favourable," he said. And there it was, in black and white: a projection of non-viability. Now Maxwell stepped in.

"Surely you cannot accept that report on the basis of the latest development?"

Gray raised his head from his copy with a puzzled frown. Maxwell continued: the scene had been entirely changed by his involvement; there could be no doubts about advertising revenue, which the report suggested might be hard to get; already he had commitments of at least £100,000 worth of advertising from top companies. In addition, we would cut the staff from six to five hundred. He invited Gray to take the report away and go through all the projections again.

Gay started to speak, but Gray restrained him with a cautionary tap on his arm. He asked for evidence of these advertising commitments. How did we propose to reduce staffing?

Maxwell replied that he would provide evidence of the advertising commitments in a few days. He had also arranged for a team of five experts from the PA management consultancy to go into the building in the morning to carry out a complete reappraisal of the manning requirements. "What more can you ask for than that? How can you now possibly publish the report?" He looked up appealingly at the pair opposite him.

Gray looked at me as though awaiting my comments. I wriggled uneasily in my seat and shrugged my shoulders. I suspected that Maxwell was lying but did not know for certain.

Now Gay spoke. "Come now, Mr Maxwell, I appeal to you not to give the workers false hopes."

Maxwell was lighting a large cigar. He paused in his sucking, waved the smoke away with an extravagant gesture and dismissed Gay's appeal with a mumbled and not wholly articulate comment about Gray, Gay, the Action Committee and the workforce being no match for his talents. They were all just a bunch of country hicks, as all Scotsmen were.

Gay exploded. His eyes flashed angrily behind his glasses. "You have nothing but an ungovernable conceit of yourself and have no respect for anyone, least of all the men in whose interest you are supposed to be concerned."

Maxwell withdrew the comments but with no real conviction. The insult remained.

FIRST THING the following morning Maxwell was on his way back to Oxford. At 10am Gray presided over his working committee to give the official finding of the study team. Cudlipp and I represented the

Action Committee and, following Maxwell's instructions, again appealed to have the report delayed.

John Duncan of PA, who was also representing the Action Committee, was asked if his organisation had any plans to send a team of management experts into Albion Street that day, as Maxwell had claimed.

Duncan looked astonished. It was out of the question, he said, now or in the near future. The team was not available.

There was no longer any question of postponement. The report was to remain unaltered. There was almost a last second reprieve when Gray, arguing with his lawyer's training that the report, although paid for by the Government and the City of Glasgow, really belonged to the workers, offered to make its publication a matter for ourselves.

But by now I had actually changed my mind. Cudlipp and I reasoned that if the report were to be suppressed, then it could be for only one reason – that it was unfavourable. Yet we wouldn't be in a position to defend ourselves by attacking it, and that could do us terrible damage. On the other hand, were it made public we could attack its contents. We issued it ourselves that same afternoon. At a mass meeting I slagged the unprofessional nature of the report and pointed out where the lack of knowledge of the newspaper industry had made the experts less than such. This was a period of our history in which I took no pride or pleasure. To survive it was necessary to attack and seek to discredit the Strathclyde team. They were honest men, every one of them. They had taught us how to think commercially and they had helped us at every turn. But unless their report and, therefore, themselves were discredited, there would be no survival for us. And we had to survive as our first priority.

Later that afternoon we were under pressure from another source. Jocelyn Stevens was demanding that we either cough up some money or leave the Albion Street building. Before his departure for Oxford, we discovered later, Maxwell had offered a strange deal to Stevens on our behalf. Out of the near £300,000 we had funded, we were to place £100,000 in a joint account to be shared between ourselves and Beaverbrook. The money would act as insurance against our damaging the property and help pay the running costs of the building. Naturally, Stevens was delighted with the proposal, but we weren't when we learned of it. Briston, hastily summoned from the university, advised us against the deal. After a short discussion among the committee members, he phoned Stevens to tell him so. There was no Beaverbrook reaction. Indeed Stevens had apparently expected this response.

ON THE following morning, three of us had breakfast with Tony Benn. At that time he was Secretary of State for Industry and was in Glasgow on departmental business. He wanted to meet us to see what our proposals were at first hand. Macgee, Hooper and I turned up at the Central Hotel at 7.45 wondering what it was going to be like to meet this controversial figure.

Personally I had then little faith in him. My own position in politics lies somewhere to the left of centre in the Labour Party but my political views are untaggable. At times I could be projected as moderate right, for example on the Common Market issue. At times I could not accept that the left wing were arguing a pure left-wing philosophy. So I suppose I could be described as being independent left. But Tony Benn, to me, was a nothing. Previously I had looked upon him as a recent convert to the left wing of the party, and I harbour a built-in mistrust of converts. Why, I asked myself, does he now flirt with the left? And I came up with the answer that he was playing for left-wing support so that eventually he could make a bid for the leadership of the party.

Over breakfast he showed not only interest in our concept of a co-operative newspaper, but also a real excitement for it. Questions were fired at us over the cups of tea, plates of kippers and bacon and eggs. His charm oiled the conversation and we were soon persuaded that we could identify in him a friend and supporter, the person we were seeking in Government circles.

That afternoon Jocelyn Stevens resumed the pressure on us. The time limit for the first option had run out. By now it was becoming well-nigh impossible to think ahead. Instead of settling down to our plans for the *News*, we were spending almost half of our time maintaining the sit-in or fighting off Beaverbrook. It was no good. We would have to fight on fewer fronts.

Stevens, through the Beaverbrook lawyers, came up with a proposal. They wanted us to vacate the main building and move to a suite of small offices across the road from the main building. Once it had contained the streets sales offices. It was an L-shaped hut with six offices, toilets, hot water and a telephone line. If we moved there, said he, our first option on the building would be extended for another three months. The proposal was put by Beaverbrook's lawyers in London to ours in Glasgow over the telephone conference system. All this was explained to me over the phone by Brian Dorman, who added that by mutual consent of the lawyers it had been taped to make the offer binding. Dorman asked me to inform the Beaverbrook management in Glasgow. Accompanied by Macgee and Blyth, I explained it all to Paterson, the Scottish chairman of Beaverbrook. The sleep-in, by this time, had been discontinued so that once our meeting was over at around 7pm I went straight home. That evening I learned that Blyth had made a hostile move in my absence. Most of the others had gone for an hour to the Dunrobin, a local pub. Over his beer, it was reported to me, Blyth fantasised the meeting with Paterson by claiming that I had met Stevens in London and that we had agreed to tape our meeting. I had done this without the committee's knowledge or permission. Mackie, it was implied, had gone too far. This was at the time of Watergate and President Nixon. The very mention of the word "tapes" aroused all sorts of wild emotions. It was unanimously decided that I would be challenged first thing in the morning.

But Hooper wasted no time that evening in phoning me at home to demand an explanation. My own surprise at the allegations was so genuine that Hooper needed no substantiation. "Well, be on your guard in the morning."

May 25

WHEN I made my explanation in the morning, Blyth's comment was, "I'm sorry, I must have picked you up wrong last night." It was an apology of sorts. But the effect of the episode was that my own credibility was breached. Though I was completely absolved at the time by Macgee, there remained an odour of intrigue which had immediate effect. This became evident when we took the first item on the agenda, which was the Stevens proposal.

After a short debate the proposition that we move to the Hut was put to the members. I must have been tired or dispirited because normally I would never have allowed the vote until I was sure of the outcome. My recommendation that we move out was narrowly defeated. There was a shocked hush. I gathered up my papers, pushed my chair back, stood up, and, feeling perfectly at ease, told the meeting that, irrespective of the vote, I had no intention of continuing in occupation of the building. A reasonable offer of alternative accommodation had been made to the committee and I, personally, had every intention of moving out.

There was uproar. Blyth was shouting something about a betrayal of the workforce, Goldberg spluttered that I was a megalomaniac. McNamara and Russell said they intended to follow me. It was a scene of confusion. But I won the argument without another vote being taken. That afternoon we started to move out of the building and into our new premises. The following day we were firmly established at our new address – the Hut. The sit-in was over. On our part it was a calculated risk to move out. We accepted that. But it was imperative to establish a new relationship with Beaverbrook. They could no longer be viewed as the ogres who had brought us so much trouble (though indeed they were). In future they would have to be regarded by all of us as business associates. Some of the committee members never quite arrived at that state of detachment. To them the struggle was always one of getting their own back at Beaverbrook and, in particular, at Jocelyn Stevens. That did little to help with the real struggle.

CHAPTER FIVE

A great moment?

SHORTLY after the move, Briston completed his feasibility report on the committee's proposals. In it, and it is a remarkable document, he compiled all the proposals we had made and linked them to the financial projections of a modest circulation. It proved our viability, given these assumptions. It was used as the submission to the Department of Industry when we applied for assistance. Once the report had been finalised, Briston approached me one day and asked if I had any objections if he showed a copy of it to Jocelyn Stevens.

It made sense to me, yet it was a tricky question. Briston had already persuaded me that Beaverbrook was probably the most likely major investor. The entire committee was aware of this and accepted it grudgingly. But it would be a different proposition to let Stevens see the submission. He was still the enemy. All this I explained to Briston.

He said: "You lads will have to grow up if you want to survive." I agreed with him. So did Russell and McNamara and a few of the others. But I couldn't take the decision to the committee because I knew it would be thrown out and it is always preferable to have no decision than a bad one. In the event, I suggested to Briston that, since he was the financial adviser to the committee, he would have to decide for himself whether or not it was in the interests of the paper to hand over a copy to Stevens. Briston correctly interpreted my decision as the go-ahead and passed the report over. Soon the information was being fed back to the committee that Stevens had somehow obtained a copy. In London one day with Gibson I admitted that I had had some foreknowledge of Briston's intentions and had done nothing to stop him. By this time Briston had gone off to Indonesia for a three-month government tour, and so I knew that he could not be attacked in his presence by some of our wild ones. But Gibson lost no time in spreading the news around that I had colluded with Briston in a betrayal.

Often I felt like resigning at this period. It was the blackest and least rewarding time in the history of the struggle. Teams had been organised to tramp round the trade union general secretaries, seeking their financial help. I didn't expect us to be treated as a new Messiah. And we weren't. The union leaders were as sceptical as our lads were euphoric. But the tragedy was that the euphoria was blunting their judgment. Soon reports were being compiled about a possible £100,000 from this union, or a niggardly £50,000 from that. You would have thought we were playing an enormous game of monopoly. But my greatest error was that I voiced my fears about the lack of realism at a committee meeting. And that almost burst their balloon of optimism.

Blyth, the hardest-worked member of the committee at this time, led a team into Fleet Street, hoping to raise cash from the newspaper chapels there. Before long he was talking about raising something in the region of £100,000 from that source alone. Macgee humorously referred to the team as "the super salesmen" as they kept feeding back the optimistic and never realised commitments of cash.

But added to fighting the phoney war, there was the real war being fought within our own ranks. On a trip to London I met up with an FoC of a chapel in the *Daily Telegraph*. He gave me a piece of advice. "Watch those people you are sending down here. They are doing your hoped-for newspaper no good. The image they are projecting of your workforce bounces between some sort of wild Marxist outfit and a Scottish Nationalist outcrop. In addition, they are spreading the word around that you are in the fight only for your own personal political advancement."

Within three days I read almost exactly the same observation, along with the reference to myself, in the leader column of the *Telegraph*. It was not difficult to guess the source but there was nothing I or anyone else could do to stop the poison.

A harder approach was made to merchant bankers, the Co-operative Bank, the Bank of Russia, to almost everyone who was involved with cash and the lending of it, but all with the same sad result. The Co-operative Bank's response was a lulu – they had no faith in the co-operative structure of our company.

Briston thought up an idea to invite various financial interests to a meeting in the Central Hotel in Glasgow. The professor gave his address to the gathering; Russell followed it up. Russell told me later that it had been going very well. The financiers were asking questions which bespoke keen interest. Then Denny Macgee decided to make a contribution. Apparently he threw his arms in the air like an actor and gave them a lecture on their responsibilities to society in general and the *Daily News* in particular. "After that their interest melted like a snowball in summer," said Russell.

NOW FOLLOWED a curious time. We had little to show for our struggles yet hope kept breaking through. Maxwell all this time stayed put in Oxford. We saw neither hilt nor hair of him for weeks on end; and he was never available to receive phone calls. His continued interest in the *Daily News*, indeed, had become a matter for speculation. Yet it was still necessary to maintain the public image. He had gone on television, radio and press, and had committed himself. We had no intention of letting him off the hook. But despite all of that, optimism was rising like the sap in spring.

From our Government contacts came discouraging noises. There seemed a reluctance to support the appeal, on the grounds of insufficient public interest. To counter this argument we launched a nationwide campaign to gather signatures of commitments to support the paper for a three-month trial period. And the response was incredible. An intensive canvass secured in three weeks more than 153,000 signatures. A meeting was arranged in No 10 to hand them over to whip up as much publicity as possible. Goldberg, our liaison man with Maxwell, phoned Oxford about our plans. For a change Maxwell was contacted. He discounted our activities as a waste of time, a characteristic treatment of anything proposed by someone other than himself. But he did suggest that we convene a press conference while in London which he would personally address. Not surprisingly, his offer of help was turned down.

On the eve of the demonstration that we were planning for the handing-over procedure I was already in London. I phoned Stevens and asked him for a further extension of our first option. To my surprise and delight he agreed, with virtually no discussion and no concessions on our part.

The season of optimism continued. I perceived a marked turning point in the struggle. Many of the early divisions were beginning to heal. Armstrong had approached me only two days previously to explain his own position. He confirmed that Blyth had been fomenting opposition to my chairmanship. He had been impressed by Blyth's record as an FoC: he had been more militant than I in my role of Imperial Father. Now he had revised his opinion. "But why didn't you declare war on him and bomb him out?"

I explained, as I had done to McNamara earlier, that this was for the committee. Unless they matured enough to sort things out, then there was little chance of either launching or sustaining the paper. He thought for a couple of minutes, slowly shook his head with disapproval and made a vulgar comment about how some people ought to be treated. But it was good to have Armstrong back in the camp. He was an unyielding customer, an unrelenting enemy or a totally loyal friend. For years he had been my muscle man.

Once, as Father of the Federated Chapel, I had had to deal with a situation where a group of clerical workers wished to exercise their legal rights and leave their union. A closed shop operated at the time. Both sides were happy with the arrangement and the management feared chaos if it broke down. I attended a meeting with John Paterson, the Scottish chairman of Beaverbrook, with Armstrong there as my deputy. The dissidents' leader asked for an adjournment in a private room. Just as I was entering it, the first of the group, I heard a dull thud behind us followed by a sharp intake of breath. I was surprised to see the dissident unionist falling to the ground, holding an area in the region of his right kidney. Armstrong stood over him. "And that's another fucking thing for you to think about while you're at it!" he growled. I didn't approve of Armstrong's industrial relations style but I now needed his support more at that time than at any other period in my relationship with him.

I felt daily more confident that we could, in the end, really make a success of launching the paper. To add to my growing optimism, the demonstration turned out a success. Around a hundred of the workforce came in two coachloads and cars, and they were on their

best behaviour. As always, they were reminded: "You must look on
the media as your greatest enemy, looking for a whip to beat you with.
Give them no help."

However, our optimism was soon sorely tested. The TUC
General Council rejected our appeal for support. They did this on
the advice of Richard Briginshaw of Natsopa, the print union
representative and therefore a voice of decisive influence, who had on
the previous day met Liddell and me at Natsopa headquarters in
London. That meeting turned out to be one of the most delicate in my
negotiating experience. At the outset, Briginshaw, a fast-talking
Londoner in whom I had no trust whatsoever, told us to give up the
struggle and look for a job. The time had come, he said, for us to pack
up. He would do absolutely nothing to help us on the General
Council.

It was a cruel and mindless attitude. Other general secretaries had
pledged us their support just so long as our own representative spoke
up on our behalf. I resented his arrogance but revenge was mine before
the afternoon was over. When we emerged from the meeting BBC
and ITV camera teams were waiting. Before Briginshaw could open
his mouth I stepped forward and said that we had had a good meeting;
and that we had found in Dick Briginshaw a good and loyal friend
who had pledged his support for us. I then turned to shake his hand in
friendship. The look on his face was one of utter astonishment, but he
did not have the courage to refuse my hand or speak against my
statement. I felt no sympathy for him.

Elsewhere the pickings were thin. Four months after the start of
our struggle our Fighting Fund stood at £140. There was no
substantial trade union support apart from a £5,000 investment from
Ray Buckton of ASLEF (the train drivers' union) and a massive loan to
the fund from the shop stewards of UCS (Upper Clyde Shipbuilders).
There was no evidence of Government support. There was no real
belief that Maxwell would deliver his money either. Some of the
workforce were beginning to drift away to other jobs, taking their
precious money with them. Morale was on the slide. How long could
we go on like this? Another hard decision faced the committee. The
trust fund was due to be wound up in a few days and the money
would have to be transferred to another fund. This was a moment of
danger, obliging us to take stock. It was also a moment of temptation,

to take your money and blow, or to take some of it out to solve an immediate cash crisis. Four months of unemployment has a bad effect on your finances.

FOUR OF us, Macgee, Riddell, McNamara and I, were discussing the worsening situation before the regular mass meeting. Riddell asserted that he was convinced we could not fail; it was just a matter of time. McNamara looked up with his mocking crooked smile. It was high time, he said, that they told the workforce success was far from being inevitable. "We've got a responsibility to tell them the facts; and the facts are that we are on the point of collapse unless something turns up."

Macgee snorted with rage. "And you, Mr Chairman (*derisively*), what do *you* think?."

I said: "If the workforce really believe that we cannot fail then we must tell them to dampen their euphoria and prepare them for the possibility that we may eventually fail."

I had seen men explode with anger before but never with quite the ferocity with which Riddell and Macgee greeted my comment. They out-shouted each other, demanding my resignation to make way for another who believed in the ultimate inevitability of success. The shouting was still continuing as I left to make my way down to the meeting in the City Hall to give my usual dosage of optimism, and appeal for more cash and patience.

At the meeting, I made no reference to the real situation but within myself decided that it would have to be sorted out soon. Half way through the meeting Irene Mackay joined me on the platform. Her presence surprised me since she was usually too busy typing or filing letters to attend the mass meetings. She had a message. Tom Band of the DTI's Glasgow office had been on the phone wanting to speak to me; it was urgent. Another half hour had to pass before I could wind up the meeting with a growing tension. The call meant one of two things – the go-ahead for the loan or the end of the road.

Then I was through to Band. I listened to his words but their meaning did not register at once. "It's all right, Allister. The Government has agreed to make an offer of the loan, but with certain conditions attached to it. You will receive a copy of the conditions within the hour."

And that was it. In the Hut, where the committee had gathered, all eyes were on me as I replaced the receiver. "We've got the loan," I said.

There was little response. Macgee was the first to speak. "What exactly do you mean?"

"I mean the Government has agreed to offer us the loan we asked for. We've won."

A loud cheer arose. We had done the impossible. Armstrong shouldered his way through the others, wrapped his arms round me in a bear hug and, his eyes moist, growled: "We've done it, you old bastard, we've done it."

Over Armstrong's shoulder I could see Irene Mackay with the tears streaming down her face. Gibson and Hooper embraced, McGowan stood in the middle of the floor, alone, with both arms raised in a victory salute. Such was the din that some of the workforce who were still finding their way from the meeting heard us from outside, rushed their way into the Hut, and wept along with us.

It was a great moment. We had stood almost alone for so long. Now Tony Benn, despite the unions' lack of support, had joined ranks with us in a magnificent act of faith. Surely the unions would rally behind us now.

Russell, ever cautious and sceptical, was the only member of the committee to show any reservations. "Let's wait until we see the conditions before we celebrate."

Within the hour the entire terms of the offer were given to us. The letter, signed by Tony Benn, said that the Industrial Development Advisory Board had been impressed, as he had been, by the Action Committee's energy and enthusiasm. But it too had concluded the project was not viable. However, he had said they would be prepared to consider our application for assistance under the Industry Act if the Action Committee were able to give certain assurances. He was now prepared to offer a loan of 50% of the total cost of the project up to a limit of £1.75m if the Action Committee could satisfy him on certain conditions. These were:

1. The Action Committee would have to find from non-Government sources 50% of the capital cost, then estimated at between £3m and £4m. Such investors would have to have seen the advice given to the Government and be aware of the risks involved.

73

2. The committee would have to have received, irrevocably and in cash, the £475,000 in subscriptions to which it had referred in its letter to him of July 3.

3. In addition, the committee would have to have received a further £500,000 in the form of equity or long-term unsecured loans from commercial sources or the general public.

4. In the case of secured loans, the lenders would have to have agreed to share available security pari passu with the Government.

5. Members of the workers' enterprise and all others providing finance would have to have confirmed that they realised that in the event of failure creditors would be ranked:
   A: Secured creditors, including the Government.
   B: All unsecured creditors.
   C: Shareholders.

6. The committee would have to have accepted in writing that this would be the only Government contribution and no further finance would be forthcoming. All providing finance for the project would have to be aware of this.

Russell's scepticism seemed well founded. The Government was willing to make an offer of cash but seemed unwilling to deliver the actual money. The conditions nailed the offer to the table. It was election year and the Scottish Nationalists were emerging in Scotland as the biggest threat to the Labour Party's superiority. Was the offer simply an election ploy? Time would give the answer to that fear. The important thing was that we had reduced the capital required to launch the paper. Yesterday we had been looking for £3.05m. Now we sought £1.3m. Was this not cause for optimism, albeit of a cautious kind?

CHAPTER SIX

Tested by failure

THE OFFER was what Briston had been waiting for. From that moment on he seemed absolutely convinced that we could not fail. Within a few days he had arranged a meeting with Jocelyn Stevens in London to negotiate the value of the building. Beaverbrook had demanded £2.55m. Our assessors had valued it at £1.4m. Our team consisted of Brian Dorman, for Boyds; Ken Barclay, from our assessors; Briston, Russell, McNamara and myself. We faced Stevens, flanked by his financial and technical advisers.

From the start Dorman and Barclay attacked Stevens ruthlessly and with a fierceness that would have done credit to an FoC. Stevens countered with the argument that there was now another party interested in buying the building and, despite all the arguments, he had a responsibility to Beaverbrook shareholders to sell to the top bidder. The argument ping-ponged for about two hours when we adjourned for a break. We were ushered into an office for a half-hour recess and to gather further thoughts on how to break the impasse.

I don't know whose office we were in, but there was a *Scotsman* lying on the desk. In it McNamara noticed a front-page story that concerned ourselves. It contained a statement by John Paterson, the Beaverbrook Scottish chairman, that there should be no difficulty for the workers to purchase the building since there was no other bidder! It was impossible to believe that our find had not been contrived – but by whom . . . ?

At the reconvened meeting Stevens's reply to Paterson's statement was a broad grin, with no comment. Barclay followed up with his company's assessment of the building's real value, reducing Beaverbrook's valuation for one reason or another. He concluded:

"And of course we must take into account the buggeration factor."

Technical terms were becoming commonplace for me but this one had me stumped. Stevens too looked puzzled. "What do you mean?" he asked.

"I mean that as long as these lads are hanging around, no other bidder could reasonably hope to make a straightforward bid without being buggered about by the workforce. This, naturally, reduces the value of the property and must be taken into account."

Stevens's response was a hearty laugh.

AT THE end of August we lobbied the TUC at Brighton. Money by this time was desperately tight and seven of our committee had to spend the first few nights camped out in tents. But unseasonable gales whipped the tents away in the middle of the night. On my way down to Brighton I had stopped for breakfast at the restaurant at Euston Station. Half-way through my meal I met up with Gregor Mackenzie, an acquaintance from my days in the Labour League of Youth some 25 years previously. He was at that time MP for Rutherglen and junior Minister at the Treasury. He surprised me with a curious question about Goldberg. Was he a wild man of the left? He had that reputation in Government circles and it was doing us no good. He advised me not to send Goldberg on delegations to meet Ministers.

AFTER PROTRACTED negotiations with Stevens, Briston had at last succeeded in reducing the selling price of the building and plant to £1.6m. A reappraisal of our cash needs showed that we were now looking for £1.4m. Then he dropped a bombshell.

"With £250,000 of the workers' money still intact, plus Maxwell's £125,000, that leaves us with around £2m to raise. Now, if the Government is willing to lend us £1.4m instead of the £1.75m they have offered, I am reasonably confident that Beaverbrook will find the remainder of the cash. But persuading the Government to part with the £1.4m might not be so easy. Although they originally offered £1.75m, they did insist that they would not lend more than 50% of the total. We would now be looking for a 58% loan, even though the actual amount of cash was less."

According to Briston, we could be only weeks from our goal, if the Government would just be reasonable. We would have to find out. Within half an hour Benn had agreed to meet a delegation of three. They would be Briston, myself and one other. But who would the other be? I waited with butterflies in my stomach as the nominations came in.

McNamara proposed Russell, my own choice. Macgee proposed that I should select my own delegation, but received no support. Gibson moved Armstrong. Then Blyth moved Goldberg. For me there was now no option: what I had to do had to be done.

I looked around apprehensively. Raising my right hand, I called the meeting to order. "Nathan, I suggest that you withdraw nomination. I have it on authority that you are politically *persona non grata* among certain Government areas of influence. Your inclusion in the delegation will be an embarrassment to the committee, to Benn, and to others in the Government who support our fight."

After a pause the storm broke. Goldberg protested that it was disgusting, victimisation. Blyth joined in but I could not make him out because Goldberg was shouting. Macgee joined in. I said nothing but waited for the commotion to pass. Eventually McNamara made himself heard in my support and my recommendation was accepted almost unanimously. It was an indication of their growing maturity. At times it would be necessary to sacrifice people's feelings in the interests of the paper.

THE MEETING with Benn was held a few days later. We were a bit apprehensive about it – and not only because of our request to increase the Government's loan percentage. To counteract continued Government comments that there was no indication of public support for our struggle, we had contacted various people in the country and asked them for a commitment to invest. By this method we had received promises of some thirty or forty thousand pounds. These activities were illegal, and we knew it. Time and again our lawyers had pointed out that we must issue a prospectus first. But how else could we ascertain if there were any public support? Now was the time for the reckoning, for the civil servants had found out.

We met, Briston, Armstrong and I, in the hall area of the sixth floor in the Department's headquarters in Victoria Road, London. As we waited, planning our tactics, we were interrupted by a voice. It was Tony Benn, hands outstretched, smiling as ever, and with that concerned look on his face that I found so engaging when speaking to him.

"Sorry, only a minute to spare, lads, I'm supposed to be at the loo. A quick word to warn you that you are in trouble with the Solicitor-General's office. You've been seeking commitments to invest from members of the general public. Now, you know that's illegal and I'm not particularly blaming you for trying to get away with it. No, Allister, no time to waste," he went on, waving aside my explanations. "The important thing now is to handle it. As you come into my office I'll deliver you a right rocket. Take it seriously, because it's in your own interests to keep on the right side of the legal eagles. And listen carefully, this is what your reply must be . . . "

Our defence was spelled out to us by Benn in detail, then he insisted that I go over it again. Next, with a hurried "good-bye and good luck", he was off again to await our arrival. Somewhat dazed, we were soon being ushered into the room where Benn was awaiting us, apparently in a grim mood, flanked by an array of lawyers and other civil servants.

He opened the meeting by giving us a prepared statement printed on two sheets. This stated that letters issued by the Action Committee, in the opinion of the department's solicitor, constituted circulars whose distribution was an offence. The matter would be considered by the Lord Advocate but in the meantime it was very important that the committee should comply with the law. The department would have to approve any further document or circular. The prospectus would have to comply with the Companies Act and drafts of it should be sent to the department.

Next he delivered a searing broadside without a trace of sympathy or understanding. I retaliated with my primed statement. Benn puckered his brow and then glanced in the direction of his legal advisers who nodded their heads in acceptance of my explanation. We were in the clear. Benn relaxed, winked his congratulations at my performance, smiled, then invited us to speak.

In his unassuming manner, Briston put our proposals. Again Benn replied with a declaration of his personal support for our struggle and promised to put our proposals before the Cabinet. Before we left he insisted yet again that unless there was some evidence of support from the print unions it was going to be a difficult task.

Time and again the message was being driven home to us that it was imperative for us to gain official union support yet our unions would do little or nothing at all. And all our appeals for help passed by unheard and unheeded.

WHILE THE meeting with Benn was taking place, Macgee and Blyth were again doing their best to destroy my control over the Action Committee. In Glasgow I had by this time reasserted my authority in the committee and was experiencing very little trouble in controlling the dissidents. But whenever I was absent either Macgee or Blyth would take the chance to attack me. In the case of Blyth, it was rarely done in my presence.

The pretext for the attack on this occasion was my recommendation that Goldberg be excluded from the Benn delegation. Macgee introduced the debate, expressing alarm at my action which he saw as yet another instance where I was attempting to usurp the authority of the committee and invest it in myself. McNamara and Russell came to my defence but the debate continued for some two hours before Hooper, who was acting as chairman in my absence, called a halt to it. It was yet another symptom of the split that had persisted from the early days. But the minority group was diminishing in numbers. There remained only three who were constant – Blyth, Macgee and Goldberg.

When a stormy and violent scene was being enacted, and that happened at least three or four times a week, I would shudder. Thousands of people were pinning their faith on us and yet we were incapable of normal civilised behaviour. The shouting and brawling could be heard almost the whole length of Albion Street. Passing strangers would pause to look.

Even in retrospect I cannot put my finger on the mistrust my enemies felt for me. Blyth was continually claiming that I was in the struggle only for my own good, that political ambition was my guiding force and not concern for the *Daily News*. Certainly in May of that year I had been elected on to the District Council of West Lothian. But that could scarcely be said to be climbing the ladder of political power, considering my majority was a mere four votes, and I had since been asked to resign as treasurer of the local Labour Party because I could not attend their fortnightly meetings with sufficient regularity.

No, my political ambitions were not the reason for such hostility. They lay deeper than that. My ability to lift the phone and speak to Members of Parliament I had known for decades was resented. My access to people who walked in the corridors of power was suspected. It was thought that perhaps I was privy to Government information that I was not imparting to the committee. This was seldom the case, though at times necessary. The entire committee could not be trusted to keep confidences and on very few occasions I had to withhold some morsel of information.

It is also probable that the trio's hostility had different origins. Blyth seemed determined to become chairman. Macgee had a profound mistrust of humankind. Goldberg's lack of a political and philosophical anchor allowed him to drift into an intellectual whirlpool from which he seemed unable to escape: he was by far one of the most intelligent members of the committee and his contribution, had it been better disciplined, could have been phenomenal.

The daily war for cash continued. Andrew McCallum, a former reporter on the *Scottish Daily Express* was loudly contemptuous of the Action Committee but tirelessly extorted hundreds of pounds from dwellers of castles in Perthshire, hard-nosed publicans in Glasgow, and show-biz personalities. In London he walked into the United Arab Emirates on a chill September morning. His enterprise eventually produced a visit to Albion Street from a sympathetic Arab press attaché – but no cash.

Ray Chard was another individual doing his own thing. Like McCallum, he was a journalist with a profound contempt for the Action Committee. Dapper, moustached, he moved into society, and persuaded the Duke of Argyll to invest. Nobody would believe it, and that caused a row and wasted much time in committee. But it was true.

THE SCEPTICISM which engulfed Chard was merely a symptom of the frustration that was gripping our members. Violent arguments were beginning to break out almost daily over trivial incidents. Crossan was accused of showing too much interest in the affairs of his bowling club. Gibson was blamed for taking a half-day off after a visit to the employment exchange. I was justifiably criticised for bad time-keeping. McNamara was censured by Macgee for attending the Celtic football match on a Saturday afternoon in preference to a debate on some long-forgotten vital topic. I clearly recall Mr McNamara's response to Macgee's attempts to censure him. He simply smiled at him with that crooked mocking smile and chanted:

> "We're crazy, we're mental,
> We're aff our effing heid."

By now there was an openness in the way we addressed each other. When you thought someone had told a lie you told him so and discarded any pretence at diplomacy. It was now not unusual for someone to tell the man sitting beside him that he was a rascal and a cheat. No-one by this time took umbrage.

The major receptacle for ill-feeling was the wage rate for the editorial department. We had by this time agreed to a wages level throughout the building. There was to be a rate of £60 for the night-shift tradesmen. Unskilled workers would all be paid 11% below this rate while journalists were to be paid 15% above it. There were differentials still to be worked out for day-shift rates. Many of the workforce were not all that happy with the differential between the others and the elitist journalists, but the majority accepted that they would have to accept the difference to keep whatever number of journalists they had.

WITHIN A few days I received a phone call from Benn. "I'm dreadfully sorry, Allister," he said. The Cabinet had decided not to allow the loan except under the conditions laid down, and insisted we would have to raise half of the amount required. Benn went on: "This was a decision arrived at after discussion, and I am bound to defend it. So don't spare me from your criticism. Now tell me, what do you intend to do? Will your lads pack up and go? It would be a great pity if they did."

"Have no fears," I said. "We'll be around to pester you and the Cabinet for a long time to come. Now we must meet the conditions laid down."

Macgee exploded when I broke the news. He waved his hands as if they were theatrical props. It was "disgusting, disgraceful, shocking."

He was "astonished." What we had to do was launch an all-out attack on the Government for its heartlessness and lack of concern for 500 men on the dole.

But he got very little support from the other committee members apart from Blyth. It was obvious there was going to be a General Election before long. If we were to attack the Government it could give ammunition to the nationalists and possibly help to return a Tory Government. There would be no support for us in that direction.

McNamara summed up. There were things in the world more important than the *Scottish Daily News*. The return of a Labour Government at that time was one of them. "If it is necessary for us to allow the Government to destroy us without our making a protest in defence, then so be it. What we must do is decide what is good for the working-class people of this country. I suggest that a Labour Government takes priority over our dream of a silly wee newspaper which might never take form anyway."

It was a mature view to hold and one which endorsed the feelings of many of the other committee members.

HAROLD WILSON, the Prime Minister, decided to launch his General Election campaign in Glasgow. Never behind the door when an opportunity presented itself, we asked for and were granted a meeting with him in the Central Hotel. It was decided to send Macgee along with me since he had attended the previous meeting, and there is always an advantage in speaking to a known face. Wilson arrived accompanied by Willie Ross, the Scottish Secretary, and some half-dozen others. We met in a small ante-room. Wilson was ebullient. The opening rally had been a great success and the Scottish audience had risen to his oratory.

Sipping a large glass of brandy, Wilson pointed out that, although the workforce had not fully met the conditions laid down by the Government, and despite the decision of the Cabinet not to waive the letter of the conditions, there was no great cause for despondency. "I tell you I still consider myself committed to supporting you and will do all in my power to help you. Willie and I together," he pointed his glass in the general direction of Ross, who smiled over at us, "have the authority to do this between us." Ross nodded his head in agreement but made no further contribution.

The brief meeting over, Ross escorted us to the door and within seconds we were making our way downstairs again.

THE SPARK of hope lit by Wilson dimmed quickly. Maxwell had gone to ground yet again, and no other cheque books were being waved in our direction. By the end of September all of us were feeling depressed. Everything had been poured into the struggle, our hopes had been raised then dashed, then raised and dashed, time and again. Briston was somewhere on the other side of the world on a government contract. Charles Graham, who was first choice for the post of editor, had decided to turn down the invitation. It was like climbing an escalator moving downwards at a speed we could not surpass. Russell even proposed a hunger strike, and it was a sign of its mood that the committee spent 90 minutes discussing it before adjourning for lunch.

It was a pleasant day. Autumn was just making its presence felt with a slight nip in the air. Seated in a public house just off Argyle Street, I asked Russell if he had had any further thoughts on the hunger strike. He looked at me sheepishly, almost with an air of a mischievous brat who had been caught out. "It seemed a good idea at the time, but now when I think about it over dinner I almost feel embarrassed. It would never work and would probably make us all look a bit stupid."

Hooper, seated at the table next to our own, and overhearing Russell's retreat, joined in. "Thank Christ for that, Jimmy." Thus ended the hunger strike before it could begin.

WE DID agree to let the workforce know of the apparent impasse we had arrived at. Over the period we had evolved a trust from the workforce that was the key of our strength. Never at any time would we tell them an untruth. Occasionally we would have to pad out the truth or, alternatively, fail to mention developments that might have destroyed morale. This time, however, we would have to let them know the real situation we were in, of our fading hopes.

One of the biggest problems our members had was going home and explaining to their wives that yet again the Action Committee had drawn a blank. The men themselves were kept constantly informed at the weekly meetings. But not the wives. They were expected to sit at home and receive the latest bit of bad news with stoic calm. That was more than could be expected. So, on this occasion, we invited the wives along so that they could share in the disappointment. To ask them to rally round would not be enough: we would have to try to involve them. Why not ask them for the commitment of even more money? With their wives attending, the members might more easily come to that decision.

The speech I made that evening was one of the most difficult and therefore one of the best I believe I have ever made. All the facts were placed before the meeting – the lack of union support and Government interest, the falling investment because of members leaving and taking their money with them or simply going broke, and the apparent conspiracy of silence by the national press; and this cold-shoulder treatment by the national press was probably the most damaging morale-sucking problem we faced at that time. The reporters were forever snapping at our heels for (so we believed) portents of impending failure but their time spent among us was seldom reflected in proportion to press coverage of our struggle. Then, having knocked our members to the floor, I raised them up again. I challenged them to step up the struggle and follow the Action Committee into taking on the Establishment that wished us to go away and leave its conscience at peace. They rose immediately and backed the committee with more than their voices.

Within 48 hours another £44,000 had been pledged and the workforce had developed a harder, aggressive and more determined mood. But those meetings, the difficult ones, always demanded a high price of me. Oh, they were a challenge all right, with the reward of seeing the men lift themselves off the ground. But after the meetings, when everyone had gone off with their batteries re-charged, I'd often lock myself in the toilet and bring up everything that was in my stomach. They left me exhausted and depressed. What if I was leading the workforce into Hell rather than the Promised Land? Had I the moral right to keep making these demands of them? Even if we did get the paper off the ground would those people who trusted in my judgment lose their money? This sense of responsibility, I believe, was the greatest weight I carried around with me in those days. I have never quite managed to rid myself of it, even to this day.

CHAPTER SEVEN

Stormy weather

ABOUT THAT time the committee's single biggest problem was the replacement of Charles Graham as editor. One thing was obvious. Without a credible editor to control the contents and style of the paper, there was no chance of any support from any source whatever. Some journalists wanted us to consider Macgee, a few others Goldberg. Neither was suitable. And there were no others who could be described as executive material. Apart from Fred Sillitto, that is.

I had known Sillitto for some 13 years or so. He was one of the friendliest persons you could hope to meet in the industry. He had been the deputy editor of the *Sunday Express* in Glasgow. Rather than move to London he had chosen to accept his redundancy and join us. Politically he seemed mildly Labour, with an intellectual view of politics. In his earlier life he had had a brief membership of the party, but after a quick baptism of disillusionment about the way the ward parties were run in Glasgow, he had opted out again and had decided to support from the sidelines. Politically he was acceptable. But would he have enough spunk to take on and lead his journalists? We couldn't know. The moment selected Sillitto, then aged 57. The concept attracted and excited him. He threw in his lot with us, committing part of his redundancy money.

He was a complete professional journalist and his professional detachment did not allow him to be wildly enthusiastic about our chances of success. Years previously, on a Saturday, an experience had possibly changed him for life. As assistant editor, he had been handed a piece of copy telling the story of a young man killed in a motor-cycle accident. The story was routine. The young man was his son, and this was how he found out about the tragedy. Perhaps as a result, he was an introvert. He chain-smoked. At meetings he tended to mumble and avert his eyes from the person he was speaking to. He was a good man, with many fine qualities, but we thrust on him the responsibility of creating our dream. It was unfair but we had no other choice.

THERE WAS little opportunity for stepping up political pressure before the General Election. Briston, returning from his overseas trip, remained quietly confident that there was no real problem. All we had to do was stand firm, hold the workforce's money and support, then negotiate an agreement with Beaverbrook since there was obviously no other bidder for the building. He certainly persuaded us that we could and probably would win in the end, simply by keeping our heads.

Our days were not wasted. It was a time for debate, discussion and self-education. We drew up a disputes procedure that would have been the envy of every newspaper in Britain. It was never put to the test. There was only one incident requiring disciplinary action and it was resolved by the Process chapel inviting one of its members to resign from his job.

All this time we were gaining a tremendous amount of public support from, I believe, every section of the community. One day I received a phone call from Archbishop Scanlon of Glasgow. He explained he was not well paid and had no cash to contribute but had prayed for us. It was a touching contribution. But despite our constant appeals the unions still did nothing to help. By this time we were looking not so much for cash as their blessing. The Scottish Graphical Association did commit its support, but the others would give little indication of either sympathy or concern. The worst feature of their attitude was their sheer indifference to our situation. Most of them simply did not care. Their indifference had various causes. The general secretary of SLADE claimed that he couldn't give his union's support, although 20 jobs were involved, because he couldn't trust our political attitudes. While he was wittering on I began to frame my response on the assumption that he had some form of intellectual misunderstanding of our position. Then he leaned forward to adjust the knot in my tie, at the same time admiring its motif. It was the standard Labour Party tie of quill, spade and torch. "And what organisation does the design represent?" asked he who had doubts about our politics.

Ken Morgan, general secretary of the National Union of

Journalists was unenthusiastic about our future and little wonder. One of our senior journalists had written him a letter seeking his support to help us create a newspaper that would be prepared to avert "the insidious threat of the National Party." Understandably Morgan felt concerned at this reference to some of our potential readers and advised us so. He was right. Our letter should never have been sent to him. It did not reflect our views on the paper's political attitudes. We did not perceive the Nationalists as an insidious threat. Further we would be a paper independently left but that the politics of the paper would be carefully concealed so that the reader would arrive at a conclusion that was in keeping with the philosophy of the paper rather than having it thrust down his throat.

October 7

THE LABOUR Government was returned with an increased majority. The Nationalists had duffed the Tories but, had our workforce not restrained their criticisms of the Government, Labour also might have suffered. Maxwell's failure to win back Buckinghamshire did give us slight concern. Had he any further use for us?

I sent a letter to the Prime Minister asking for a public statement of commitment. I indicated that our paper, while seeking help from the Government, promised no support in return. All that was promised was the creation of an independent newspaper at liberty to criticise the Government whenever it thought fit. Three days later I got my reply:

10, Downing Street
22nd October, 1974

Dear Mr Mackie,

Thanks for your letter of 21st October. I am being kept closely informed of the progress of negotiations on the *Scottish Daily News*. The offer which the Government had made is proof of our sympathy, and support for this project. I understand that you have discussed your revised proposals with the Secretary of State for Industry this afternoon and you may be assured that the proposals which you have put to him will be considered with urgency.

As regards what you have said about the editorial line, it had been my expectation throughout that your newspaper will uphold the traditions of free and independent journalism which we in this country value so highly.

Yours sincerely,
(signed) *Harold Wilson*

Once we had restarted our political pressure, Briston began burrowing away at the Beaverbrook organisation through a constant stream of phone calls. Again it was a time of rising hope and expectations. The civil servants, for the first time, seemed more friendly than before. Their attitude previously had been hostile and at times almost rude in its curtness.

TONY BENN agreed to meet us yet again to discuss the latest developments. Briston and I took Sillitto with us to show him off to the Minister. As usual, Benn was seated at a large wooden table. Behind him I noticed a large trade union banner representing the General Workers' Union. Asked where he had got it from, Benn grinned sheepishly and admitted that he had, in fact, stolen it or rather "borrowed it and then forgot to return it."

He assured us he would back us in every way he could but he would find it increasingly difficult to gain Cabinet support as long as our print unions would not stand up and be counted. "That is your greatest weakness . . . Once they support you other unions will back you to the hilt."

He continued: "I noticed in one of the nationals that you will be printing a paper of the Left. Do you think it wise to shout your policies from the rooftops? Wouldn't it be just as easy to say that you will be radical in your point of view rather than left? No doubt it will mean the same thing but then you will appeal to a broader section of the public that you will need."

I could hardly wait to tell him of the letter I had sent to Wilson. Benn was delighted that we had asked for his support but did not offer ours in return. "Excellent, absolutely excellent; that's the correct thing to do."

Then he asked a question he said had been worrying him. "What about Maxwell . . . is his money secure . . . can you control him?"

Briston forestalled me before I could say anything indelicate. "I can quite appreciate your concern," said Briston. "In fact we all share it. But I do believe that at the end of the day the workforce will manage to control him all right. I have every confidence in them."

Benn was resting a giant mug of tea in both hands. He rested his elbows on the desk before him and looked at all three of us. His comment was a slow silent nod.

WITHIN A few days, and despite our plea to Benn, we received formal notice from the Department of Industry that the Government would not allow us the loan until every *i* had been dotted and every *t* crossed. This time they went further and told us the reason for their decision was the lack of union support for our struggle and the apparent lack of interest from the Scottish public in the paper.

Some members of the committee threw up all the old-hat proposals – occupy the building, step up the aggro, seek support from other political parties, especially the SNP. Briston was unperturbed. The attitude of the Government meant we knew where we stood. What we had to do was contact Stevens at Beaverbrook. "There is no other bidder for the building, I'm absolutely certain of that. So they are going to be landed with a monster that no-one really wants, unless it is ourselves."

I looked round the table at the faces of the committee members. How different it was from when Beaverbrook was the enemy. Perhaps Jocelyn could be a lifeline instead of an executioner. We had travelled a strange journey.

Briston continued: "I shall propose that Beaverbrook make up the cash to us by underwriting the prospectus. They'll agree to it, I know they will: they have no alternative. And in this way we shall be fulfilling the terms of the loan to the letter. The Government could not possibly hold the loan back from us once we have raised the cash, but just so long as they hear nothing of it beforehand."

BENN AGAIN agreed to meet us, this time at his home in Holland Park, London. A lived-in house always has soul, when children's toys are scattered around, a guitar is left on a couch, a teaching manual is on the piano's music-rest and a single woollen stocking lies under an armchair. The room wasn't clinically tidy but it was friendly and warm. Mrs Benn, tidying up, apologised for her husband's lateness. The four of us – Macgee, Blyth, Sillitto and I – sat down to wait.

Within minutes, Macgee was playing a selection of light music on the piano. The rest of us looked self-consciously around, desperately wishing that he would wind up before Benn arrived. But he didn't. Benn, when he came, asked about our cash commitments. We reassured him but he said he wished there was more evidence of the public support we claimed.

The discussion continued for about another 45 minutes in the same vein and then we left to meet a delegation from the Scottish Labour Group at Westminster. Before we did so Macgee embarrassed us again. He told Benn we could not give the public a sample of our product as if it were a biscuit. He nibbled off a bit of an imaginary biscuit, let it roll around his face, smiled in delight, and then nodded his head in approval.

"Perhaps you ought to be getting along," said Benn.

BRISTON HAD lost no time in meeting Stevens. He got a verbal commitment of agreement with his proposals. It was by now the beginning of November and the Government had set us a deadline of December 1. If we could not meet the conditions in full by that date, the offer would be withdrawn.

Although it was another time of optimism, life was difficult for all of us. At times I felt I could no longer cope with the pressures. My wife became pregnant and had to stop working, thus ending a major source of income. I received no unemployment benefit for a nine-week period because I was unable always to turn up at the dole queue at the appointed time each week. I was making at least a weekly trip to London and elsewhere, and more often I went twice a week, always by rail because we could not afford the air fare. Eventually I learned to sleep in short doses, particularly on the return journey.

I stumbled on a slightly dishonest way of getting the journey north on the cheap. I had bought a cheap day ticket, hoping to catch the last train home for which the ticket was valid. But I missed it and was stranded without enough money to make up the full fare. The only thing to do was to reserve a sleeper and chance my arm when the attendant came round. He spotted the disparity but fortunately recognised me and let it pass with some friendly banter. Two weeks later, in the identical situation, the trick would have worked again had I not encountered the same attendant. My embarrassment was such that I never again tried to economise in this way.

Economising with the Fighting Fund became an obsession with all of us. Liddell, who held the purse strings, grudged every penny he doled out, then demanded receipts for what little we did spend. In London we allowed ourselves £2.50 for overnight accommodation – and that was in the winter of 1974–75. Somehow or other we always survived, though at times we had to slum it a bit. Once five of us spent the night in a room in a small hotel near Kings Cross. But these journeys breached the dole rules. I lost benefit, even though I was probably working harder for the right to work than anybody else in Scotland at the time.

Eventually I managed to make my appeal before the Bathgate Appeals Tribunal. The chairman read out my claim and the reason for its refusal given by the insurance officer. This said that although I had claimed to have met various Government Ministers, MPs, etc, I had provided no evidence of this.

I was bemused. But before I could comment the official sitting beside me interrupted. He introduced himself as the new insurance officer of the area. The report's author had moved up north and it was now the opinion of his office that I had been unfairly dealt with.

The chairman looked puzzled, then relieved. He said: "It's nonsense to talk of lack of evidence. I have personally watched him, along with almost everyone else in Scotland, meeting Mr Wilson and other politicians. It's just as well your predecessor's been posted elsewhere. It makes the case an awful lot easier to deal with."

In the end I received all my back payments. The money came in just before Christmas and I blew the lot on a second-hand grand piano. It was something I could ill afford and it meant going without later. But it was still worth it.

THE TIME had come to educate the entire workforce about the financial structure of our company. Briston addressed a mass meeting, armed with blackboard, chalk and a sheaf of notes. He told them that £2.4m had to be raised. Half would come from the workforce, Maxwell and Beaverbrook. Once this had been raised then the Government would offer the loan of £1.2m.

Briston next emphasised to the members the need to push on with the prospectus. For months Patrick and Dorman had been working on drafts. It had been a very difficult operation because of the hostility of Treasury officials. They had insisted that it should contain all the damaging reports that had been made – Strathclyde, the Industrial Development Advisory Board, the Industrial Development Unit. Had they agreed, and these documents had been printed in full, the prospectus would have been very costly and would have been ridiculed with their inclusion. After months of haggling a compromise was reached where we agreed to refer to the reports and indicate that they would be available for inspection. So obstructive were the officials that at one stage Patrick and Dorman threw up their hands and said, "No more." They would have no part in issuing a prospectus that ridiculed the company seeking financial support. Not until then did the officials relax their demands. It was almost as if they had been seeking this point of ultimate resistance.

THE BRISTON lecture had been filmed by STV and I was afterwards asked to the studio to be interviewed. The following morning Macgee demanded that the committee take a look at TV coverage. He spoke of his deep concern about the publicity I was receiving. He demanded that more of the committee, including himself, be allowed to make public pronouncements.

He got no support but I agreed with him. I *was* receiving too much publicity and the struggle was becoming personalised. But it was no fault of mine. The media came to me because I was chairman. I had tried to get them to use other speakers and with some success. Goldberg, Armstrong, Briston and others had made good interviews. Sillitto, too, had made the occasional appearance. But his naturally reserved personality had not made much impact.

In one way or another I was frequently being projected as a hero, but no image could have been further from reality. No leader can have ever been as unheroic as I. At times, had I known how to withdraw gracefully, I would have done so. But the ghosts of preceding generations held me captive: the 1820 Scotland Martyrs; John McLean; the shop steward movement of the Clyde; the Upper Clyde Shipbuilders. They all held me in their grip and demanded a service that was frequently grudged but never refused.

At times I felt that far from leading the workforce I was myself being led. There was an uncanny chain of unlikely coincidences. Our workforce were held prisoner because they had no other jobs but they had cash. Our former employer, it seemed, could not dispose of the building. For the first time in years there was a Labour Government. Tony Benn, possibly the only man in the Cabinet who had the courage to support us, was in the key office. Briston and Russell formed a partnership that offered perhaps the best financial advice available in Scotland. Boyds the solicitors decided to support us. Maxwell had gambled at a time when he needed publicity. There were my own connections in the political scene. Everything seemed to conspire irresistibly. So strong was the coincidental chain of events that I could feel optimism even when things were at their worst. I had a sense that there was a pre-ordained reason for the setback; it was only a preparation for later progress.

SILLITTO HAD been asked to prepare an outline of the paper's contents and his presentation followed Macgee's outburst. There was a flurry of layouts and a brief introduction about a brave new design that would capture the Scottish imagination. The outline of content and design was disastrous. He was giving us page for page the old *Scottish Daily Express*.

Lindsay said: "If that's the best you can do then heaven help the *News*."

After a few minutes of tortured silence, Sillitto proposed an essay competition for children, with weekly prizes.

There were no comments. This was our promised land of journalism, with new standards for honesty and investigative work.

We emerged with our confidence much diminished. But Sillitto was our editor. We had to accept him and seek out a successor as soon as the paper got off the ground.

November 16

THE COMMITTEE now tore itself apart with its worst display of internecine fighting during this part of the trouble. The occasion was the election of the Works Council. It was absolutely essential that the right council should be chosen. There were to be six of us from the Action Committee. If these included Blyth, Goldberg and Macgee, I had no doubt, it would herald the end of the fight. Their obsessive suspicions – of the lawyers, accountants, Briston, myself and anyone other than themselves – frequently brought everything to a standstill. Briston saw their influence as destructive and said he would have to consider his position if even two of them were elected. The committee would not survive a month if they were required to make decisions.

Blyth and Goldberg wanted to postpone the elections. Russell put the case for going ahead, adding that I would have to be on the council *ex officio* as chairman and the person recognised as leader of the workforce. In his opinion the lawyers would have nothing to do with the prospectus if I were not included. In response to a question from Macgee, I said I agreed, not because I was indispensable but because I was chairman.

Goldberg, Macgee and Blyth blew up in a magnificent rage. Macgee was screaming at the highest pitch of his voice that lawyers had no say in the selection of councillors. But just as we were reaching for our pens to vote, Macgee and Goldberg leaned across and started to whisper in Sillitto's ear. He nodded, and then Macgee requested a half-hour adjournment. They retired to the room Sillitto was using as an office.

Russell beamed. "You know what's going on, don't you?" I nodded my head, beaming too. The Action Committee had agreed that initially only shop-floor members should sit on the council. Macgee and Goldberg saw themselves as potential editorial executives; promotion would rule them off the council.

After 30 minutes I went in search of them. Sillitto looked at me in surprise. Goldberg frowned. Macgee looked furious. He said: "I've no doubt you'll be happy to learn that you won't have to worry about Nathan and me. Neither of us is standing."

I looked pained, enjoying the moment. "Denny, you have it all wrong. I'm not happy. I'm absolutely delighted. Your selection would have been a disaster."

I topped the poll with 13 votes out of a possible 14. McNamara, to his astonishment, came second with 12, while Armstrong and Blyth had 11 each. Russell and Lindsay completed the roster with eight votes each. Russell deserved more. His contribution had been enormous and it was becoming evident that he would have a major role in the days ahead though increasingly he was being regarded by his fellow-journalists as a traitor: this was because he put the concept of the co-operative first.

THE EDITORIAL set-up was fast becoming the surest way of provoking a fiery debate. Their outlook as a group was totally incompatible with my personal concept of a co-operative. Their executive set-up was a rehash of the Beaverbrook days, with payments for added responsibilities. One day Sillitto argued that you had to pay top wages to get the best men. Then he stated that all the top positions had more or less been filled with unemployed journalists already available. That seemed to contradict his argument. The appointment of Chard as managing editor ruffled Armstrong. He had no management experience and did not seem qualified. Such appointments should surely be ability-related. My worry was that Sillitto, having handed out the various top posts, would have nothing attractive left to offer senior journalists from outside. And we badly needed new blood.

Bit by bit all the appointments were made. To a man they were those that had been nominated by the planning board some eight months previously. They were not an impressive team. There was so far no mention of Goldberg or Macgee. Sillitto was evidently reserving for them the posts of deputy editor and assistant editor. It worried me a lot – particularly the prospect of the immature and unstable Macgee as deputy. I warned Sillitto that if the appointment were made I'd move heaven and earth to have him sacked as editor. But the planning board had won the day.

George Welsh had taken over the job as journalists' FoC. He was made deputy chief sub. On the day after the appointments he called a chapel meeting where it was decided that executives, once the paper was launched, would not work beyond their agreed hours unless paid for it. This was a sickening betrayal of earlier commitments. When we were told of the decision we simply said that any executive who was dissatisfied could leave immediately. As it turned out, the threat never materialised.

But despite the self-destructive aspects of our struggle, our hopes were still on the up. Briston and the lawyers kept plugging away at the prospectus. And then at last it was ready, agreed to by the Department officials, and all that was needed was to set the date for its launch. We tentatively agreed on the week between Christmas and New Year. At that time we hoped to gain public sympathy convertible to cash.

Then Maxwell re-emerged – with a vengeance.

Allister Mackie speaking at the Scottish Daily News *press conference*
(The Herald)

A demonstration and march held in Glasgow in February 1974. The marchers include
Allister Mackie, Fred Smith (General Secretary of the Scottish Graphical Association),
George Reid MP, Jimmy Reid, Hugh Brown MP, Margo McDonald, Johnnie
Beattie, Alec Ferry (General Secretary of the AEU) and members of the Action
Committee (Rolf Walter)

Allister Mackie during an address to a mass meeting of the workforce
(Christopher Davies, Report, London)

Allister Mackie at a public meeting in London with Jimmy Reid
(Christopher Davies, Report, London)

Allister Mackie flanked by Tony Benn and Robert Maxwell at the Scottish Daily
News *meeting in the* Daily Express *building in Glasgow on 13 April 1975.* Daily
News *staff are in the background*
(The Herald)

Allister Mackie greets Tony Benn and Robert Maxwell
(Scottish Daily News)

From left to right: Fred Sillitoe, Robert Maxwell and Allister Mackie
(The Herald*)*

A Works Council meeting. From left to right: Alister Blyth, William Bargh, Nathan
Goldberg, Jimmy Crossan, Robert Maxwell, Allister Mackie, Eric Tough, Jimmy
Russell and Fred Sillitoe
(Scottish Daily News)

Allister Mackie and Robert Maxwell with members of the Action Committee en route to a mass meeting of the workforce. This picture was taken on 28 March 1975, the day the prospectus was closed

The first encounter between Robert Maxwell (middle) and the workforce at a mass meeting held in the basement of the Daily Express *building on 15 May 1975 (Rolf Walter)*

Robert Maxwell at the offices of the Daily Record *in 1986 (The* Herald)

Allister Mackie
(Allister Mackie)

CHAPTER EIGHT

Manoeuvres in the rain

AFTER TRYING to contact Maxwell for several days we eventually succeeded in having a telephone conversation with him at his home in Oxford. His message was brutally unambiguous. If we published the prospectus without his having some say in its content then he would consider his commitment at an end.

We arranged for a delegation to meet him at Oxford on Friday, December 20. The arrangement was arrived at on the afternoon of the same day. Goldberg was an obvious choice. He had a rapport with Maxwell. Russell, because of his financial expertise, was asked to accompany him. Within two hours they flew from Glasgow Airport, and on the Sunday Russell phoned me to give an account of the expedition.

They had turned up at eight o'clock as arranged. By the time they arrived at Headington Hall they were soaked to the skin and frozen to the bone. At least, they consoled themselves, they could look forward to a meal, a drink and a bed to lie in. But when they rang the bell it was a long time before the door was answered. They were told by a servant that Maxwell had retired for the night and had left word that he was not to be disturbed. They had to walk all the way back to Oxford in the pouring rain and put up in a small hotel.

In the morning, when they arrived back at the house, Maxwell lost no time in warning them that the committee must on no account issue the prospectus without his consent and approval. It would have to include the Beaverbrook underwriting commitment. He wanted to go through it with a fine tooth comb. But that would have to wait until after his Christmas holidays which he was spending aboard the QE2.

It was a real setback. We had been poised to issue the prospectus.

But Maxwell had us in his grasp and he knew it. Over the phone I tried to change his mind. But he said: "If the prospectus is issued without an underwriting it will make me look ridiculous in the business world. I'll be taken for a real patsy, the only person who is willing to invest." Nothing could persuade him to change his mind.

Before the week was out reports began to percolate that Maxwell had informed the DTI of the Beaverbrook underwriting intention. Their attitude was as we had predicted. Almost certainly they would interpret the raising of the cash with the Beaverbrook underwriting arrangement to guarantee it as not being within the terms of the conditions of the loan. Goldberg phoned Maxwell on the QE2. His message was that we should arrange a meeting with the officials towards the end of January. He would personally negotiate with them on our behalf. All would be well, he said, now that he had taken a more active interest in the company. A preparatory meeting with Maxwell was arranged for January 7.

January 5

TWO DAYS after my wife Pat had given birth to our son, Goldberg and I met Maxwell at Oxford. From the start Maxwell made clear his intention to dominate our meeting. Again we sat at the large table in the working lounge. Although he had been a thorn in my flesh for some time, I always found that if I could get Goldberg away from the influence of others he could be a great asset. Copies of the annual report of Pergamon Press were lying on the table. Maxwell was fondling them as though they were alive. He invited us to read them. Look, he said, at the profit level and the interest that had been paid to shareholders. "This is just a small example of what I can do for a company when it is needed. In addition, I pay good wages and involve the workforce in every respect. That's what I believe in – make the company viable. There can be no security for your members unless the company is viable. For a start, as a condition of my loan, I must have the assurance that there will be no wage increase for the first 12 months. Do I make myself clear?"

Goldberg was doubtful. "I think you'll have trouble there, Bob."

Maxwell turned to me. "Allister, you understand these things better than Nat. Explain the situation to him."

All the while I had been thinking about the commitment. As long as we got our money out of him at the end of the day we could promise Maxwell absolutely anything at all. If we had control of the company then Maxwell could do nothing to upset any decision the Works Council might make. A commitment to Maxwell at this stage was absolutely worthless.

I told him he was quite correct and that a commitment from the workforce would be a necessary prerequisite. "We'll put it to the members, Nat, and I'm sure they'll agree." I asked Maxwell if there were any further points.

He looked at us both quietly, his lizard eyes darting from one to the other. A few seconds passed before, carefully choosing his words, he said: "Yes, there is another point and a very important one."

He paused, as if measuring in his mind the extent to which he could go. Goldberg and I looked at each other. We both knew what was coming.

Maxwell continued: "To be a success our co-operative will require public credibility. Otherwise you will not raise enough finance to qualify for the DTI loan. The public must be assured that you will make the paper a commercial success, making the correct commercial decisions. In other words I am saying that they will be looking for someone they will have faith in.

"Now, Allister, you have done a magnificent job. You have nothing but my admiration. No-one else in Scotland could have done as well and in such adverse circumstances. But tell me what is your experience in management? None. And this is where I can be of help. I shall sacrifice my valuable time down here in Oxford and come up to Glasgow to help you run the paper. But obviously I cannot do that simply as an interested party. It wouldn't work out that way. No, I shall have to take on the responsibilities of chairman. You, Allister, can become my deputy and together we'll make a success of the paper. I shall be responsible for all the financial decisions, while you will take care of important matters like labour relations. Now what do you think of that for an offer? What more can anyone do for you than I have proposed?"

In no circumstances could we agree to his being chairman, or to being responsible for the financial and commercial decisions. That couldn't possibly be a co-operative, by any definition. Yet if we were too blunt about things it would probably give him the pretext we still believed he was looking for to back out of his commitment. Goldberg's mind was moving in the same direction. I could read the puzzled expression on his face as he struggled to find the correct words. He spoke first. The position of chairman, he said, really ought to belong to one of the workforce. Otherwise the public would accuse us of not being a co-operative. "Let's be very careful about our public image. It will be needed to raise an awful lot of cash . . ."

Maxwell interrupted. "No, I insist. I must make sure that my investment will be well looked after and that can be done only by making me the chairman of the company." He demanded my comments with a hard stare.

I replied: "I can appreciate your feelings. We all agree that your role in the co-operative will be a vital one if we are to survive. None of us has had any experience in management, nor in making commercial decisions. This we acknowledge. So, you see, your position within the company is quite secured. But I agree with Nathan, that you must not be *seen* to be in command, even though you will be effectively."

Maxwell looked at me for a spell, then at Goldberg, seeming to wonder if I were taking him for a ride, as I was doing. Then he seemed to dismiss the possibility with a quick shake of his head. "Well, since you put it that way, I suppose we'll get by with some alternative arrangement."

The crisis had passed. Maxwell had been promised nothing and his commitment stood. I would much rather have told him where to put his money and be done with him. But my responsibility was to the workforce and their needs, not to my personal feelings. We needed his money and I was prepared to let him mislead himself in whatever way was necessary to secure it.

The following day I reported back in Glasgow. The Action Committee endorsed our handling of the meeting but with the resolve that, whatever the outcome of the negotiations, Maxwell would never be given executive control of the paper. The decision, like the resolve, was unanimous.

Goldberg stayed in London for the DTI meeting, but I hurried home for my obligations as a new father. On the Thursday I met Dallas and Patrick and travelled down to London with them. We met

Goldberg at the DTI office in Victoria Street, where the meeting was scheduled for 2pm. At five past, there was no sign of Maxwell. We gave him another 10 minutes before writing him off. At the very last moment he came breezing in, with neither apology nor reason for his lateness. We had some difficulty in finding the right room but when we did so we were astonished to find it packed with civil servants. Goldberg whispered to me that they had come to see Maxwell perform. And he didn't disappoint them.

From the outset he demanded that the Government pay the money immediately, even though we hadn't raised the total amount that had been a condition of the loan. The senior of the civil servants told him there was no chance of that happening.

Maxwell responded that we would soon be issuing our prospectus. We intended to advertise the issue in various national newspapers. Not the prospectus, simply an advertisement stating that it was being issued and inviting members of the public to invest.

A bespectacled young woman, the department's legal adviser, was asked for her opinion. She said: "It is not permitted under the Companies Act . . . "

"Rubbish!" snorted Maxwell. He rose from his seat and dashed across the room to rummage in a wastepaper bin in the corner. He found a copy of the *Financial Times*. "You will find adverts in here where companies are raising cash with simple little adverts. Why can't we do it?"

"Because these are existing companies, trying to raise extra cash."

He took another long look at the *Financial Times*, then tossed it away in the general direction of the bin.

"We don't need these silly little adverts anyway. But what I really want from you is your reaction to a deal that I propose to do with Beaverbrook. What will your reaction be if I can secure from Beaverbrook a commitment that they will be willing to underwrite the issue of the prospectus? Now, no doubt you will be thinking that they wouldn't be crazy enough to make that commitment. But supposing I did manage to get them to make it, where would you stand then?"

The chairman smiled inscrutably. "When that happens, if it does happen, we shall of course look at our position, but not until there is the Beaverbrook commitment." He showed no sign that his

Department had already been informed of the Briston-Stevens agreement.

During an adjournment Maxwell phoned Sir Max Aitken, owner of the *Daily Express,* to make an appointment for a meeting that evening. While Maxwell was phoning Patrick furrowed his brows and looked worried. "You can forget about Briston's underwriting arrangement now. Maxwell has killed it stone dead. The Government will never agree to it now that Maxwell has raised it officially and at this level. They knew about it previously, but at the unofficial level, so they could turn a blind eye to it. But now that they know officially, they are being forced to make a policy decision. And I'm certain that the decision will not be made in our favour."

THAT EVENING Goldberg and I accompanied Maxwell to the appointment with Sir Max. We waited outside in the car as he kept his rendezvous. The reason for my not being involved was the delicacy of the situation. Were Beaverbrook to be seen to be supporting us officially there would be a loss of confidence among the staff in their Manchester office since, perhaps, their own jobs would suffer.

At the meeting Sir Max verbally recommitted Beaverbrook to underwriting the issue of our prospectus. When he rejoined us, Maxwell let us know with a thumbs-up and a wink that the negotiations had gone well. "Keep it to yourselves but he has agreed with me that Beaverbrook will provide the underwriting as long as the news does not become public. What do you think about that for negotiating? £150,000 worth of a commitment and negotiated just like that." He snapped his fingers and beamed.

Perhaps a little leg-pull might bring him back to earth. "If we pull it off, I'll arrange for you to get a knighthood."

He gripped my knee with a firm grasp as he seriously and slowly shook his head. "No, Allister, I'm not looking for a knighthood or any of that sort of recognition. If it's decided that I am to receive some sort of honour, well, good and well. But I shan't be looking for one, but it was considerate of you to think about it just the same. You see, all I want is to be able to help. I come from a very poor Czechoslovakian family. We were peasants and for years as a boy I did not possess a pair of shoes . . . But it's such a long time ago. Things are different for me now . . . A lot has happened since then . . ."

He dried up with his reminiscences and spoke very little for the rest of the evening. I felt guilty because he had naively misinterpreted my humour.

THE NEXT few weeks passed in an agony of apprehension as we waited for the Government officially to make up its mind whether or not to accept the underwriting arrangement. We had moments of optimism but mostly we braced ourselves for the disappointment which the Government was preparing carefully so that it would not lose face. Maxwell paid us another visit and underlined to the committee that his concept of a co-operative was where a person was appointed to run the company and then left to go ahead and do it on his own. The co-operative principle became involved only when the workforce wanted to remove him. We suspected that he saw himself as the appointed person; but irrespective of who the person was we could not accept the concept.

Next he demanded, again as a formal condition of his investment, that the workforce commit themselves at a mass meeting to no wage increase for a 12-month period, and that the following year there would be no more than a modest 10% increase. But by this time we had agreed to agree to almost anything in the knowledge that once we got the money out of him we'd run the company as we saw fit. At times we would consider our own morality in respect to Maxwell. Were we right, we would ask ourselves, to take the money under false promises? Perhaps we were rationalising when we persuaded ourselves that Maxwell's money was got from the working class anyway, so any money we got out of him was only going back to where it belonged. This debate on the morality of our actions troubled, I know, quite a few of us; but we had to get the money to launch the paper, and if Maxwell wanted to gamble his £100,000 in the chance of taking control, then that was his concern. It was like a gigantic game of poker.

It was during this period that we appointed our general manager. After the mass meeting, which Maxwell had asked for, he stopped me as I was going back to the Hut.

"Make arrangements to come with me for lunch," he said. "I am interviewing someone from the PA for the position of general manager. If you like you can bring someone with you."

And that was it. No indication that he was going to appoint anyone, no consultation, no reference back to the Action Committee. He was off before I could say a word of protest. Lunch took place at the Albany Hotel. There we were introduced, Maxwell, Sillitto and I, to Eric Tough. To be frank, I was not at all impressed by Tough, not at first, that is. He seemed to be efficient. But he knew little about newspapers and somehow or other I got the impression that he could be easily pushed around. Perhaps that was what Maxwell found attractive in him, for before the dinner was over he had offered him the position of general manager, again without consulting either Sillitto or myself.

The responsibility of reporting the whole incident back to the committee spoiled my meal. My position was extremely difficult. The committee members had agreed I must go along with Maxwell enough to get the money out of him. Against my grain, and everyone else's, I had done that; but this was another thing – committing ourselves to accept a general manager who might well be sitting in Maxwell's pocket. I told Maxwell that I could not accept the appointment and took the trouble to tell Tough the reason for my hesitancy. He understood perfectly.

After the meal, on the way to the airport, Maxwell made it clear that he expected the committee to support Tough's appointment but that, if not, there was someone else in London he had in mind. All this I reported to the committee. But I recommended that, irrespective of Maxwell's reasons, we should accept Tough. He was then a man around the early fifties, prissily tidy in his appearance and with rimless spectacles. He seemed to have an enormous amount of managerial knowledge. I argued that because he lacked experience in the newspaper industry he would have to rely on the Works Council. And once Maxwell was back off to London, Tough, having had no previous tie-up with him, would come round to our side in the confrontation.

It was unanimously if reluctantly agreed to endorse Tough's appointment. Within a week he had left his position with the PA and joined us. After two more days we were satisfied that far from being in Maxwell's pocket, he was against almost everything he stood for.

Despite its misgivings, the committee agreed to announce

Maxwell's appointment as co-chairman. It was a hard decision for us to take, and one which we hated ourselves for taking. Yet there seemed little alternative. We offered him deputy chairman, associate chairman or other titles. He refused them all, finally "conceding" his acceptance of the co-chairmanship. "You can continue to be chairman," he told me. "In the interest of the public image I suppose I'll have to accept that."

In the meantime we learned from various sources that the Cabinet had reached a decision. A phone call to Benn clarified our position. The situation, he told me, didn't look too good. The Cabinet was not happy with the Beaverbrook underwriting, though no official decision had yet been taken. The reason for their reluctance was, first, if the project collapsed Beaverbrook would not really have lost anything since we were possibly the only likely purchaser for the building. Next, they were unhappy about Maxwell being involved with both Beaverbrook's and his own underwriting arrangements. They had been of the opinion that Maxwell was to be an investor, not an underwriter for the prospectus.

I interrupted. "But Maxwell is an investor. He is not there to underwrite. His commitment to us is that he will invest."

There was a slight pause and then: "Are you sure? We understand from some source or other that his commitment had become one of being willing to underwrite, not to invest. Obviously something has to be cleared up before we can go any further." He suggested that we arrange to meet.

The conversation left us wondering just what Maxwell had been telling the DTI officials. We wasted no time and arranged the meeting for the following afternoon.

CHAPTER NINE

Calvinists and presbyterians

January 28

THERE WERE four of us on the delegation, Russell, Armstrong, Macgee and myself. Now, our argument to the Government had been that the Beaverbrook underwriting operation had been no more than an insurance cover that would not really be necessary. At that time our finances stood at:

Workforce:	£200,000
Maxwell:	£100,000
Beaverbrook secured loan:	£225,000
Beaverbrook unsecured loan:	£500,000
Public commitments:	£ 90,000

This made a total of £1.115m, leaving us only £85,000 to raise from the prospectus. The public commitments came from members of the public, trade union branches, chapels and a few national unions who had indicated their support. There was every reason for optimism as we read the situation. Macgee's main responsibility in the committee had been to collate and keep a tight record of these commitments. To our knowledge he had made a good job of it and had every commitment carefully filed away. Now his files would play a vital role if we were to persuade the Government to rule in favour of the underwriting. He claimed we had £90,000 and he honestly seemed to believe it.

The meeting with Benn was not all that good for us. We went in strong at first and Benn was very impressed with our claim about public commitments. "You certainly have much more public support than I had anticipated. You don't happen to have the files with you?"

Like the conjuror picking out the traditional white rabbit, Macgee flourished the files from his briefcase and handed them to the Minister. Benn looked at them casually and then passed them to a civil servant, asking him to tally the figures to confirm our claim.

There was a hiatus of small talk as we waited for the files to be scrutinised. Then the civil servant returned. "Is this your complete file?" he asked. I looked at Macgee and then nodded.

"In that case," he said, "you have only in the region of £58,000 – certainly nowhere near the £90,000 you claim to have."

There was nothing I could say or do. There was a loud silence while Benn looked at me queryingly, prompting an explanation that I could not give. Guilt must have been staring from my face as I thrashed around for a reasonable defence.

"There must have been a mistake. I can offer no other explanation."

Macgee avoided my glance. The meeting wound up with our agreeing to take the files back and go over them again in Glasgow. But it left us with the feeling that for the first time the Action Committee had been caught cheating. Macgee was tackled the instant we were out of Benn's room, but it was too late then.

We waited for some sort of hostile reaction from Benn, but it never came. In the meantime we resorted to our tested formula of pressing the Government for a favourable decision – a demonstration in London and a lobby of MPs. This, we hoped, would be our last one and we intended to make it our greatest success. Half a train was reserved for our delegation and at Euston we gathered up in fours or fives, then headed by three pipers set off for the Embankment. I found myself sandwiched between Sillitto and Tough. Yes, Tough. Eric Tough. A man who had given up a post that brought him in a guaranteed £10,000 a year to join us in our protest for the right to work.

It was a good turn-out. On arriving at the Embankment and to conform to local bye-laws, we dispersed and made our way to Westminster. The lobbying over, we had a meeting with Tony Benn.

Well, not all of us. Tough, Russell, Gibson and I made up the delegation. We met in Benn's office in Westminster and he was well attended by a retinue of civil servants and Ministers. As ever, Benn listened with great understanding and patience, even though the discussion was interrupted by division bells. On one occasion, as he was running for the door, he turned round half-way out and joked: "Just keep the Department running until I get back."

Eventually we did succeed in getting a meaningful conversation going. At one point he gave the opinion that we had handled the underwriting wrongly. He said we should have negotiated the principle of it with the Government before announcing Beaverbrook's acceptance of it. I told him that we had learned not to trust the Government. "They haven't shown us much sympathy to date and we believe that they will seize on any pretext for turning us down."

Benn replied: "I suppose you know best yourselves what you are doing, but I must confess that I thought your handling of the underwriting hasn't worked to your advantage."

February 14

BENN PHONED me to tell me of the Cabinet's decision on the underwriting. They could not accept it. I told him that we would then launch the prospectus as quickly as possible, and test the public reaction. He seemed unhappy at the suggestion and cautioned me against it. I never did quite comprehend his reluctance on this occasion.

When I reported to the Action Committee the first reaction was speculation on whether Maxwell would use the occasion to back out of his commitment. And his reaction was as disappointing as we had feared. "We'll launch the prospectus immediately and we'll include in it a criticism of the Government for refusing to accept the underwriting." It was a silly piece of advice.

In this atmosphere of uncertainty we travelled to London to meet Maxwell in his flat in Montpelier Square. There were six of us in the party: Tough, Dorman, Armstrong, Briston, Russell and myself. We turned up at ten in the morning and there was immediate disarray. Maxwell was not there, nor had he left word where he was. After another half-hour we traced him to Headington Hall, and again, as on a previous occasion, without apology or explanation he suggested that we get down to Oxford as quickly as possible.

Not one of us believed that Maxwell had overlooked the meeting. I was convinced that he was playing a game with us, first of all to disorientate us and then to secure a psychological advantage by holding the conference at his home in Oxford.

For this meeting I had gone out of my way to make sure that the correct delegation had been chosen. Armstrong was there for his strength and ability to attack Maxwell. His rough ruthlessness when he handled Maxwell, or any adversary, was savage and almost approached the uncivilised. Russell, on the other hand, was cold, analytical, hostile, suspicious and thus perhaps even more brutal than Armstrong. They were a perfect backing for me. I believe that Maxwell feared the three of us more than he did anyone else at that time. My role was to reassure him that the environment remained favourable for his investment yet give nothing away in return. But his mistrust of me was beginning to show through.

We gathered again round the oblong table in his working lounge. Maxwell opened the meeting with a few grumblings about the Government and the weather. Then he referred to his underwriting now being in doubt.

"What underwriting are you referring to, Mr Maxwell?" It was Dorman.

The extravagant smile, the raised hands. "My own, of course. You all of you know that I have agreed to underwrite the prospectus to a maximum of £100,000. Why do you ask that question?"

"Because," replied Dorman, "there is no question of your making an underwriting. Your commitment is one of a straight investment . . . If you wish to withdraw from that commitment you have the duty now to say so."

After some more discussion he suggested he take legal advice. He phoned a QC friend, who ruled in favour of Dorman's interpretation. As we reconvened, Maxwell did not seem very happy with the news. But he mumbled: "In that case, let me have a look at the prospectus."

Dorman, knowing that he had temporarily gained an upper hand, primly advised him that the prospectus was complete and ready for issue. The Department officials had passed it, the Action Committee had passed it, and no good could possibly come from a further delay.

But Maxwell said: "If I'm committed to investing £100,000, then we'll rewrite it and it'll be a good one. I'm well experienced in the matter of issuing prospectuses."

We went over that prospectus, yet again, line by line, changing a word here and there, shifting an emphasis at another point to exaggerate the importance of the part Maxwell had played in the struggle to set up the paper. But nothing changed fundamentally until we reached the part that dealt with the price of the paper.

"It will have to be a 6p newspaper. A 5p newspaper would be ridiculous in this time of rising inflation." Armstrong was not easily persuaded. He pointed out that the Action Committee had agreed on 5p. But privately I agreed with Maxwell and that you should never underprice a commodity unless you intended to reduce its quality. I said I would put it to the committee with my recommendation. He gazed at me uncertainly, as if wondering again whether he could trust me. Then with a grunt he got back to the prospectus. He insisted on a wage freeze for a year, followed by a maximum of 10% after the first year, unpaid overtime for the first three months, and various other matters which now escape my memory.

We agreed to them, not because we meant to implement them necessarily but because we all believed we would have removed the source of the demands from all effective control of the company by the time the promises would have to be met.

BACK AT the Hut, on the Monday morning, I was about to make my report but was interrupted by Hooper.

"Tell us the whole truth, Al. We're entitled to know. Blyth has been telling us that you have a job lined up in local government and that irrespective of whether or not the paper gets off the ground you'll be all right."

I felt sick in the pit of my stomach. Blyth was fingering his spectacles. He had heard it at his union branch, he explained. He trailed off uncertainly as he caught my eye. I suggested that in future a member should be present before wild allegations were made and then made my report. The resentment of Maxwell's bullying tactics was evident in everyone's face. But the members accepted his conditions without enthusiasm and with a continued determination not necessarily to implement them apart from the 6p price demand.

That afternoon Maxwell, accompanied by Dorman, paid a visit to Jocelyn Stevens in Fleet Street. And with it he almost found the excuse for opting out of his commitment. I have never had a report of the meeting but I do know that he demanded that Beaverbrook invest another £150,000 in place of the underwriting once the prospectus had been closed and the cash raised. And with his demand came the blackmail that he would not invest any cash until he had their agreement. Had not Stevens yielded to Maxwell's demand I am convinced that he would have walked away.

DAYS WERE spent rehashing the prospectus to exaggerate Maxwell's importance. One morning we were interrupted by the arrival of Kenny Grant, a former *Express* proof reader and now the father of the caseroom chapel. He was boiling with indignation. He waved a leaflet we had produced for shop stewards in the West of Scotland. The caseroom, he said, was very worried about the phrase "left of centre" in it. There was some discussion, but this flashed a danger signal to all of us on the Action Committee. Perhaps we, in the isolation of the committee, no longer represented the feelings of the others. No force could induce me to launch a newspaper with opinions contrary to working-class interests.

Could the same be said of my colleagues? McNamara, Armstrong, Crossan, Russell, Gibson, Liddell, Hooper, McGowan and lately Goldberg were the only members that I could trust politically. Already Macgee had argued that perhaps we should look at the possibility of an SNP-orientated newspaper to capture the market.

How did the workforce think? That was the thought that bugged me. McNamara was convinced that the journalists were not to be trusted politically. In my view they could be trusted just as long as someone else did their thinking for them. Journalists were to me like actors. Once the role had been written for them they would play the part asked of them. Most were capable of writing for the *Morning Star* on Monday, the *Guardian* on Tuesday and the *Daily Telegraph* on Wednesday. But these papers had a recognisable identity and the journalists knew what was expected of them. And this was where I feared we would fall down. We had no history and therefore no identity.

Two days later we sat down, this time with Maxwell for company, to thrash out further details of the prospectus. Our philosophy was simple. The co-operative would be in the complete control of the representatives of the workforce but it would be run from day to day by the professional management. The overall policy of the editorial would be agreed to by the Works Council but there would be no interference with the nightly contents of the paper. For example, we agreed that the paper would oppose entry to the Common Market. Three of us were against the paper's policy – Maxwell, Russell and myself – but the vote was arrived at democratically. There would be no sides taken on the Northern Ireland question other than the side of sanity. On the question of Scottish government we were unanimously opposed to the SNP line. But these three issues apart, the editor had responsibility to establish a reasonably radical identity.

Maxwell was fast becoming a major obstacle to our idea of the co-operative when he attended our meetings. He was like a one-man male-voice choir, bursting into our normal caution with the most outrageous and commercially suicidal ideas that anyone ever made. I became convinced at this stage that there must be more successful businessmen who are lucky than there are who are good.

Some of his ideas had our hair standing on end. He wanted to offer founder investors the right to buy the paper at half price for the first two years plus a 20% discount on advertising rates. Apart from its being a doubtful commercial decision it was impossible to operate it. He kept on producing ideas like rabbits out of a hat but we unanimously agreed that not one was worth pursuing, and we told him so. Though we kept rejecting his ideas he made very little protest. He would shrug his shoulders as if to say, "At least I tried."

That same afternoon a meeting was held in the lawyers' office to take another look at the prospectus, all by Maxwell's demand. Maxwell presided over it like a Chinese Mandarin issuing instructions to the lawyers as if they were in his pay. Patrick was having a rough time.

Gavin Boyd, the senior partner, entered the room, smoking his pipe.

Maxwell appealed to him. His colleagues were "just a bit too presbyterian."

Boyd replied: "If you think they are presbyterian then I assure you that you would find me positively Calvinist."

Armstrong sat with a face like thunder, refusing to take any part in the meeting. Russell asked Maxwell impertinent little points designed to display his hostility to him.

At length Maxwell gathered some of the agreed amendments into a bundle and asked us all to leave the room as he had some important business of his own to attend to. We trooped out, grumbling to ourselves, into an ante-room. Armstrong was the last to enter, having picked up some activity going on in the room we had just left. He was furious.

"That bastard is interviewing Jimmy Galt for the job of advertisement manager. I'm telling you. We'll have to put a stop to this. He thinks it's his paper already."

Our temperature rose further as Galt left to be followed by Douglas Ferguson, presumably for his interview for the job of circulation manager.

We redoubled our resolve to remove Maxwell at the first opportunity, once his money had been secured. But all this was concealed from the workforce. It was a bad time for the Action Committee. On some days we were so oppressed by the sense of being manipulated by Maxwell that we discussed giving up the entire struggle. But our public standing remained high. We were seen as a group of workers who had fought against the inevitability of unemployment with a stubbornness that appealed to the dour Scottish character. The Scottish Nationalists also found our struggle attractive. We were Scottish and never slow to boast about it. They knew that we would not serve their cause but, to their credit, this consideration seemed to be disregarded when set against our service to our country. In fact the Scottish Nationalist town council of Cumbernauld set the ball rolling by deciding to invest £500 in the paper. At that time the old authorities were being phased out to make way for the new regional and district councils, and there were tidy sums tucked away in various funds. These had to be disbursed but many councils who decided to invest were prevented from doing so by the intervention of Willie Ross in his capacity as Secretary of State for Scotland. Only a few of the investments were allowed.

Still Maxwell played the game of holding back the prospectus for trivial amendments. We were nearing April 1, when the Government offer of the loan would expire. His tactics were discussed daily. Finally Macgee said it was evident "our friend from Oxford" had no intention of investing "one brown penny." He would string us along until it was too late. Then he would walk away, blaming the Government. "But he is the guilty one and we must tell everyone so. We must decide to issue the prospectus and force Maxwell either to invest or face the opprobrium of walking away from us. But he dare not walk away. His public image would be finished for all time."

It was a short speech by Macgee and one of the best he ever made. We decided to go ahead with the issue. But Maxwell beat us once again. We had to have his signature to the prospectus before it could be issued – and within 48 hours he had flown out to Moscow on a business trip. We had to await his return.

The time was not wasted. Patrick asked for a full meeting of the council to go over small points for the Articles of Association. One of the clauses some members had wanted included was to the effect that only shop-floor members would be allowed to sit on the Works Council. By this time it made little sense to me since it would single out management and foremen as second-class members. In a co-operative everyone should be treated as equal. Rather than remove traditional practices this would just turn them on their head. Patrick advised against it. After a debate, never bitter, his advice was accepted.

The next point seemed to most of us to have already been agreed. This was that there would have to be a division between the executive (the Works Council) and the unions. A person could not be both a councillor and an FoC. How otherwise could the shop floor oppose a council decision? How could an FoC represent the interests of his own department and the company at the same time?

The exclusion received my unqualified blessing and the support of most of us. Blyth and Goldberg opposed it. Macgee was hesitant. As was his habit sometimes, he walked about as he spoke and he left us somewhat confused about his position. Goldberg said he knew I was quite correct but was going to vote against the exclusion because of a "gut reaction."

Tough was amazed. "Are you telling me that you are voting against the motion even though you support it?"

A nod of the head from Goldberg. The vote was carried by a large majority. But Blyth was unhappy with the result. He brooded but when he did respond, two days later, it almost brought the entire struggle to an end.

The next day proved one for steady nerves. Briston came into the Hut to break the news that Maxwell, before leaving for Russia, had told Dorman drastically to alter the prospectus. On the phone Dorman, his high-pitched voice adding to the sense of crisis, confirmed that Maxwell now wanted to include a refutal of the Industrial Development Report which had found the project unviable. His money would not be forthcoming if we did not agree, though the Department had already refused permission for such a step. In addition, he was demanding the inclusion of a guarantee that the workforce would receive at least 50% of the profits, a statement that we had negotiated a deal with a Russian newsprint company (of which Dorman had no knowledge), and commitments from potential advertisers. Maxwell also proposed that he should be executive chairman in charge of policy-making, finance and commercial decisions. My responsibilities were to be confined to chairing meetings and acting as PRO man for the council. Eric Tough was to be described as the chief operative and Maxwell the chief executive.

I was stunned by Dorman's report. I had been expecting something like this but not a naked seizure of power. At last he had come out into the open. Either we would have a paper on his terms or no paper at all. But it could not be. No force in the world would persuade me to accept Maxwell's conditions. We would fight him even if it meant destroying everything in the process. All this I conveyed to the meeting. The members agreed and decided to meet again next day, Sunday.

CHAPTER TEN

Confrontation by phone

IN THE morning I presented my analysis of the situation to the committee. I told them I intended to phone Tony Benn to inform him of the situation and to ask if the Government would allow us to use the Beaverbrook money in place of Maxwell's. Briston said he had been in touch with Tough, who had stated his support for the committee in its stand against Maxwell. We could rely on Tough when it came to the bit. That made the whole crisis seem worthwhile. Macgee strode up and down, waving his arms, occasionally brushing a grey mane from his eyes. He launched into a prolonged attack on Maxwell. He proposed we call an immediate meeting of the workforce and expose him.

But this was no answer. The Government would have to be sounded out. When I phoned, Benn sounded alarmed. He advised me to phone Maxwell in Moscow and see if he would back down as he had done in the past. He thought it unlikely that the Treasury would allow us to use the Beaverbrook money as a substitute. It took no more than 20 minutes to get through to Moscow 203 9408 and then Maxwell's voice came through loud and clear. But I kept on complaining about the line so that Maxwell spoke loudly and slowly. It was the only time I had stooped to taping. It was not our normal style but we were in abnormal circumstances. Maxwell simply repeated all the points he had made to Dorman.

He said: "You know, Allister, I've never been happy with this arrangement of our being co-chairmen. Really I ought to be the chairman, and then you'll be my deputy chairman. It'll work far better that way, take my word for it. Yes, that's what we'll do."

A difficult task confronted me. I had to persuade him to withdraw his every demand but leave his money intact. I managed it by feeding his ego.

"You really don't do yourself justice," I said. "You must surely realise by this time that we don't have the expertise to run the business ourselves. I can't understand why you must insist on all the *i*s dotted and the *t*s crossed. If we were to implement your suggestion we could lose an awful lot of public and trade union sympathy and financial support. And I'm sure you don't want that to happen."

He took a while to answer. But I said nothing, choosing to put the onus on him to speak first. I felt that I could beat him that way.

"I suppose, when you put it that way, that what you're saying makes sense. All right, then, leave that part as it stands. But as for Tough's position . . ."

On every point he raised I bantered with him until after almost 40 minutes we had won back every one. By that time he was becoming more and more crusty and terminated the dialogue with an abrupt demand to speak to Dorman if he were available. But Dorman's scruples would not allow him to use the recorder.

But I had won. There was no point in hiding the fact. Macgee shook both my hands vigorously, almost pumping the life out of them. "You've done it, Allister. Brilliant. Now we're all set for the prospectus and the history books."

Again it was a sad fact that the one thing guaranteed to unite us was our universal mistrust of Maxwell. Now we could get on with the vital step of issuing the prospectus. We had only another three weeks left to do it in. Every minute was precious now. Maxwell had left us none to spare.

ON THE Monday morning there was a purposeful feeling as we gathered round the table in the Hut. We were there for business and we intended to get on with it quickly. Blyth had missed Sunday's excitement and it emerged that he was still upset at losing the vote on Friday. By this time and with Sunday's spectacle safely behind us, most of us had quite forgotten Blyth's objection to the inclusion of the Article excluding Works Councillors from being FoCs. It seemed to be totally irrelevant. However, its relevance was soon thrust on us when Blyth announced his resignation from the Works Council as his protest. I pointed out to him in a manner that was intended to be both appealing and reasonable that his decision would delay, fatally, the issue of the prospectus. And that we had already run out of time. Blyth persisted, accepting that he was prepared to scuttle the entire project if he did not get his way.

Uproar broke out but at length Armstrong, by virtue of his superior lung power, managed to make himself heard. "I make it quite clear that if the committee gives in to Blyth on this issue, I shall resign."

McNamara said: " . . . And I'll be joining Charlie." He rose to leave. I leaned across the table and held him by the sleeve. "We'll work something out, Jimmy, it's not the end."

The argument raged all day, at times almost coming to blows. Impasse was reached. When we resumed next day there had been no overnight change.

At length when it became evident that no compromise was possible, I decided that I could not be party to the collapse of our struggle. Blyth stood alone, no-one supporting him. I turned rudely to him and said: "All right, this time you win." I agreed to remove the exclusion but warned him that from then on I'd be watching his every step.

ON HIS return from Russia, Maxwell wasted no time in arranging a meeting with the committee at the Hut. He again emphasised that control of the committee should be handed over to him.

"Tell me," he asked, "how many of you know what cash flow means? Raise your hand if you do."

At that time we had been adjusting our cash flow needs continuously over a five-month period. Briston had involved most of us when he had been preparing the feasibility study the previous year and our cash-flow updatings had been re-appraised some five or six times since the first projection. Only McGowan indicated his knowledge, then, embarrassed at seeing himself alone, slowly lowered his hand.

"Well," said Maxwell, "I'll tell you what cash flow means." And he did. On winding up he made an overt play for control.

"If you were to engage me on a full-time basis, do you realise that my services would cost you between £50,000 and £100,000 a year? Do you realise just how valuable I am to your company, and how lucky your company is to get my services for nothing?"

He beamed, but our impassive faces gave nothing away. Sensing our lack of enthusiasm, he changed his tack and asked why Nathan Goldberg and "Danny" Macgee were not among the directors. I was immediately concerned that he felt he had the right to have an opinion on the composition of the Works Council. Why did he want the two journalists on the council? Indeed, how had he found out they were not on it? On the road home that evening I discussed it at length with McNamara. Our conclusion was that someone was telling Maxwell everything that was going on in the committee.

Other members of the Action Committee were beginning to show the same concern. Gibson was the first to state it openly. On the morning of the launch of the prospectus, Friday, March 8, 1975, he said it was quite obvious that some members of the committee were in regular contact with Maxwell. "I don't know who they are but I make it clear that if they are found out they ought to be kicked out immediately." His comments were heard in an uncomfortable and uncharacteristic silence.

The rest of the day proved to be one of the longest of my life. A mass meeting was held in the full blaze of publicity. A well-attended press conference was next on the agenda followed by a frenzied dash to the airport: because of an electricians' strike we had had to hire a small six-seater plane to take us to London and another press conference organised for us at Westminster by Maxwell. Since the London papers had been well represented at the Glasgow session, I could not see the point of it. But off we set. There were Tough, Sillitto, Goldberg (in his capacity as press officer), Maxwell and myself. The journey down was a bit of a nightmare with storms all the way. We were a little groggy by the time we got to Heathrow where we were met by two of Maxwell's cars. I joined Maxwell in his Rolls with, I think, Sillitto. We were due at Westminster in 30 minutes but, in the 5pm congestion on the M4, there seemed no way of doing it.

Maxwell, sitting beside his chauffeur, kept pushing him to overtake, first on this side, then the other, or mount the kerb. Eventually the exasperated driver could take no more.

"Look, guv'nor, if you think you can do any bleeding better, take the wheel yourself."

Maxwell tapped him on the shoulder. "Drive on to the hard shoulder, I want to talk to you."

As the car drew up, Maxwell opened the door to get out and said: "Get out of that fucking seat. I'll drive it myself."

Unperturbed, the driver turned to him. "You won't do any fucking better, but I'm not going to break my neck for your sake."

With that he pushed himself angrily out of his own door and changed places, grumbling audibly about his employer's bull-like temperament.

Maxwell's performance was certainly more effective. He drove all the way on the hard shoulder. Once we had run out of motorway, he drove through every red light on the way to the Houses of Parliament. There we had little to add to what had already been said in Glasgow.

THE FOLLOWING three weeks passed in a maelstrom of activity and excitement. Never before had an entire workforce been engaged in raising money from the public and trade unionists in such a manner. Our determination was born out of the certain knowledge that failure would mean a continuous spell of unemployment and a complete waste of 15 months' effort. Four teams were organised under team leaders. They were given geographical areas and a performance league was drawn up. Tom Clarke, a compositor, was the leader of his team. A quiet-spoken man, he had shown throughout the struggle a talent for raising cash in the most unlikely quarters and from the most unlikely people. Now he showed inspired leadership. Soon his members were sending in reports of investments that had the other teams staggering. Crossan was put in charge of the Aberdeen team. With expenses of £4 per day, a battered van and a blind faith, the Aberdeen brigade invaded almost every work area in the north-east of Scotland. The response was less than encouraging.

I had a sore conscience with some of my private worries. They started when Charlie Auld of Bo'ness, the first member of the public to commit himself to an investment, asked me to make his £100 up to £1,000. I didn't feel all that certain his money was secure. On top of that, Tommy Wood and Eddie Knight, both fellow West Lothian district councillors, decided to invest £100 each. I knew they couldn't afford the cash yet I couldn't afford to refuse it. As the campaign continued more and more people, out of personal friendship, made their investments. When one came from my brother I almost sent the cheque back. My only consolation was that I had had no part in their decisions, had made no personal approach.

The prospectus was published as a two-page advertisement in the *Scotsman* of March 11. From all corners of Scotland members of the public dipped into their pockets. Union branches throughout the UK made their contribution. Local authorities made what investment they could within the law. Some of the national unions joined in.

At last the morning of March 28 dawned – the last day of the issue. Today Macgee's special responsibilities as book-keeper for the Action Committee would come to an end. To him had fallen the task of receiving, recording and acknowledging the cash. He had handled this demanding job like a professional.

By nine that morning he was securely established in the secretary's office, getting ready for the last-minute rush that we knew would come. Mrs McColl, the cleaner, waved her goodbye as she put on her coat to face the winter cold. The committee at an early stage had agreed to ask her formally to be the first to re-enter the main building when and if the time came. The choice of the cleaner for the honour had been because, for us, she epitomised the co-operative side of our struggle. As she clattered her way down the steps of the Hut, she passed a middle-aged workman wearing a cloth cap and with his dungaree bottoms secured by cycle clips.

Macgee recognised that here was another act of faith and hoped he realised the minimum subscription was £25. The man fumbled in his pockets and pulled out a bundle of dirty fivers. Then more came from another pocket, then another. Soon the table was littered with them. Slowly, incredulously, Macgee counted until he reached a thousand. His hand shook as he signed the receipt; he was so overcome that he could find no words for his gratitude. For the stranger, we kept a warm spot in our hearts.

BECAUSE OF an industrial dispute at Glasgow Airport, Maxwell landed in Edinburgh where I met him. His Moscow fur cap bounced above the heads of the other disembarking passengers. On the way to Glasgow he bombarded me relentlessly with questions.

"What is the latest return? . . . What do you hope to get out of it – a seat at Westminster? . . . What shall I say about the workforce? . . . "

The questions flowed all the way to Glasgow where Maxwell asked me to make for the Albany Hotel rather than Albion Street. The diversion annoyed me because we were running late but he said he had some business to do there. At the hotel we made for his suite where I was surprised to find waiting two *News* journalists, Ray Chard and Allan Saxton. While Maxwell unpacked they explained they had come to a personal and private arrangement to lend him £11,000 to help with any shortfall in the investments.

With growing apprehension I asked them if they fully knew what they were doing. "Don't worry," they said. Maxwell had promised them their money back from late investments and they had a letter to that effect.

I confess I was overwhelmed by their faith in the newspaper. But this was the kind of worker involvement I did not particularly care for. For two workers it was a big commitment. In the excitement of the following days I forgot about this incident and was later severely criticised in the Works Council for my failure to report it to them at the time.

IT WAS around mid-day before we arrived at the Hut. The Action Committee was gathered and their hostile expressions spoke for themselves. Without waiting for an invitation Maxwell took over. He said: "We are agreed that Mackie will attend to the day-to-day running of the paper, while I will look after the financial and commercial decisions." Again he asked us if he knew what his services would cost. What more did we desire of him? There was nothing more. And so he continued:

"Every member of the Works Council will write a letter of resignation . . . Immediately . . . It will be signed but undated. Then if any member of the Council publicly speaks out against any decision by the other members of the council, the date will simply be added, and the resignation will take immediate effect." It was, he added, a condition of his investment.

There were protests but we signed the pathetic little scraps of paper anyway. I heard Russell whisper to McNamara that they were worthless. He goaded Maxwell into signing too and soon they were collected up into an envelope.

Maxwell pressed on. "A further condition of my investing is that you will agree that we produce an evening edition of the paper as well as the morning edition."

The idea had been ours a year ago. We had discussed it over many days and had felt it held the key to our future. But some of us were a bit concerned about the *Evening Times*, published by Outram. We wanted to make a success of our co-operative but not at the cost of the jobs of our colleagues on another newspaper. It was a problem we would face once the new paper was established.

Seeing no objections, Maxwell added: "I mean the evening edition will go out from the first day of publication."

This time the reaction was more spontaneous. Liddell, normally quiet and hard to upset, shouted that Maxwell was asking for the impossible. Everyone joined in with their protests. But Maxwell sat back, unconcerned. Again we had to concede but in the knowledge that it was beyond our capacity. Apart from anything else we were concerned about the prospectus. We had raised cash from the public on the commitment to produce a morning paper. Among the contributors were staff of the *Evening Times*. The fourth demand was that we put the needs of the paper above our union loyalties. Although no-one really attempted to stand against it, equally no-one accepted it. We sat dumbly and let it pass unchallenged.

The final condition seemed trifling. He was to be called "The Publisher". This seemed comic to us. We were not going to stand in his way. Titles are for fools. We would have called him "Majesty" had it appealed to his whim.

NEXT THE FoCs and those of the branch officers who had turned up were given the same treatment. During this meeting a Glasgow businessman, David Agnew, turned up to add to his original investment of £1,000. The unfortunate man was asked to wait in the outer office while the haggling went on. I approached him to apologise for our discourtesy and then managed to extricate Maxwell who told him: "There is a shortfall of £134,000. I am willing to invest up to a maximum of £125,000 but no more."

Agnew seemed almost embarrassed at the situation he found himself in. It was like a madhouse, full of hubbub and arguing. Despite that he decided to top up the last £9,000, putting in place the final piece of our jigsaw.

Maxwell immediately phoned DTI officials in London to tell them the money had been raised and to start the machinery for making the Government loan.

Meanwhile I found Briston bristling with indignation. "He's screwing all of you," he said. "Keep a careful eye on him and don't waste any time trying to do deals with him."

Armstrong was even more outspoken. "Let's face it, he's only doing what we expected him to do anyway. I hate the bastard because he treats us as though we were dummies. But just you wait. The dummies will sort him out before long."

CHAPTER ELEVEN

Easter in Paris

SOON ALL business in the Hut was settled. The workforce had been waiting with diminishing patience since 2pm in the City Hall round the corner in Candleriggs. They were becoming restless and worried. By 3pm rumours were spreading that Maxwell had refused to come across with the extra money or that he had agreed to the cash but with impossible conditions attached. Shortly after 3pm we managed to get Maxwell out on to the street for the short walk down to the hall. There was a further delay as he postured in front of TV cameras, boasting that his £125,000 investment had made it possible for the 500 workers to return to work after being on the dole for so long. He made no mention of the £11,000 loan from the two journalists or the extra investment of £9,000 from Agnew.

Our reception in the City Hall, at first apprehensive, soon soared to a crescendo when I announced that we had raised the cash. Not until the tumult had died down did I get the chance to let them know that Maxwell's investment was conditional. It was like throwing a bucket of water on a friendly, dancing fire. As Maxwell rose to spell out his conditions, I looked at the grim faces around me on the platform. I hated Maxwell for turning an occasion for celebration into one for worry and concern. It was unforgivable for him to do it at this time when we had earned the right to be happy. As he went over, point by point, the conditions he had laid down, demanding that the workforce endorse every one before he would move on to the next, the looks on the faces of the workforce, transformed to anger or bitterness, hurt me more than anything else during our history.

Later we were invited up to Maxwell's suite by way of celebration. But I can think of no-one in the committee who was in the mood for it. FoCs and others had been invited, among them Kenny Grant of the caseroom. At one point he said: "As I see it, Mr Maxwell, it will be our main responsibility as FoCs to defend you against those of the workforce who intend to criticise you." Maxwell's face lit up, he nodded enthusiastically. He had found an ally.

Maxwell and I then headed for Albion Street where we were to meet John Paterson, chairman of Beaverbrook in Scotland. I had been meeting him on and off for some 13 years and it would be a reasonable comment that we had evolved a trust and respect for each other. At this time I hoped he would lay out an opinion on our future.

He did. We had, he told us, a guaranteed success in the production of the paper. The management structure and workforce would ensure that. But we stood little chance, he feared, as long as we had the existing journalists. "They are good enough men but they lack the quality you will be needing. In fact, by and large, they are the dross left by Beaverbrook."

No matter how you looked at it, the success or failure of the paper was in the hands of the journalists. If they failed, we all failed.

When I arrived home my wife was packing our cases in preparation for a ten-day holiday which Maxwell had fixed up for us, to be spent in his flat in Paris at his expense. The reason, he said, was that he was concerned about my health and certainly I wasn't in good shape at the time. When the Action Committee was formed my hair had been a mixture of red and grey; now it was a distinct white. At home I would find it impossible to relax. If I watched television for more than five minutes I would slide into an irresistible sleep, more like a coma, from which I would stir after 10 minutes or so with a terrifying sense of disorientation. It was frightening but I was afraid to consult my doctor in case he insisted that I rest. The other members of the committee took a realistic view which Macgee summed up. "Obviously he wants you out of the way so that he can take control. Even so you must take the holiday. You've had a rough passage, and you need a break." And so it was agreed: I was to spend Easter in Paris at Maxwell's expense. I left Armstrong to take charge in my absence.

Saturday morning in the Hut was like the morning after Hogmanay except that our hangovers were emotional, for we were stone-cold sober. Perhaps the council and Maxwell could work together but I doubted it. On one side was a group dedicated to an idealist concept of a co-operative. On the other was an absolutist who ran his own company with the autocracy of a Victorian capitalist.

At our morning meeting Maxwell told us that he had appointed Fred Dench as advertising director. The news upset us more than a little. We had planned to appoint Jimmy Galt as advertising manager. Dench was a former Beaverbrook man but he was around 70: we doubted if he could stand the pace. What worried us, too, was that Maxwell had made the appointment off his own bat to an office of his own creation. It was perfectly normal, he said, for a newspaper to appoint an advertising director. "There's no point in arguing the point. I've already committed the company."

The first big blow-out came to life. We were all at it, telling Maxwell that Dench would not have a vote or a place in the council, that the staffing of his department would be strictly controlled by the council and that its expenses would be subjected to the same tight control and scrutiny as other departments. All this Maxwell accepted with a tired raising of his shoulders and a mumbled explanation.

Our next brush came when we formally agreed to ask Bob Dallas of French & Cowans to take on the post of financial controller pending the appointment of a permanent person. Dallas had already agreed to do the job for us and had tentatively arranged his release. Maxwell tried to stop the appointment, insisting that he would send somebody from Pergamon. This we rejected but Maxwell didn't press it.

On the Sunday I flew to Paris from Edinburgh Airport with my wife and son of three months. Paris was cold, depressingly so, and the cost of living was prohibitive. The flat was above the Pergamon bookshop. It was unpretentious and the only sign of Maxwell was the RM insignia on the bedclothes, towels and cutlery. After a few days walking the streets with the child in a push-chair, I decided to visit a friend who lived in a farmhouse near Caen in Normandy. On the Sunday I returned to Paris and got through by phone to Russell in Glasgow. He advised me to come back at once. "Don't waste any time if you want the paper to get off the ground at all." Maxwell's insistence that we produce an evening paper was holding everything up. First we didn't have enough staff. Even if it were possible, he said, the unions would never allow us to do it because it threatened jobs on the *Evening Times*. Eric Tough, he added, was worried about Maxwell. Ever since we had allowed him to call himself Publisher, he had taken that as our agreement that he should run the paper. "Already he has told Eric and Fred Sillitto to report to him direct in everything."

I promised to leave first thing in the morning. As we were packing at around 9am the next day the phone rang. It was Maxwell, asking me to get back to Glasgow as soon as possible. "The way they're farting around with this evening edition," he said, "they'll never get the paper off the ground. To make it worse your friend Emerson (the NGA organiser) is creating hell about the staffing now. Get back there and see what's to be done."

By evening I was home again. Next morning I reported to Albion Street where by this time the workforce was back in the building. The council got down to business. Tough made his report. It fell short in every part because of the evening edition. It could not be done. It was madness. McNamara moved we postpone its consideration until the daily had been successfully launched. Everyone agreed. All we had to do was let Maxwell know and that wasn't going to be pleasant.

When crises were in the offing in the Beaverbrook days my tactic had been to raise the temperature to boiling point as quickly as possible. It had proved successful because it tended to prevent the adoption of unworkable compromises. I crossed the road to the Hut where our only phone line was. Our first call was to the lawyers' office. Dorman assured us that Maxwell could do nothing at that stage to cancel his investment cheque of £150,000. The cheque had been actioned and the money deposited into our account.

I then called Maxwell at his home in Oxford. He listened impatiently to my report. I told him the decision was final and irreversible. Abruptly he told me to put Tough on the line. Tough then put all our arguments to him.

Maxwell's voice could be clearly heard. "Since you are incapable of carrying out my instructions – instructions I have specifically given you – I now expect your resignation and immediately. Now put Mackie back on."

His tone changed immediately when I reintroduced myself. If it couldn't be done, he said, it couldn't be done. "Now we must drop our plans for a morning paper and concentrate on producing an evening one. That's where the money will be made."

I couldn't believe my ears. There was no place in Glasgow or the west of Scotland for another evening paper. We were totally committed, legally, morally and in every other respect, to a morning paper. Maxwell was crazy. I promised to put his plan to the council but warned him I was not hopeful.

Shortly after dinner-time on the Wednesday we had the full council convened. In addition to the six elected council members there were Maxwell, Tough, Sillitto, Briston, the luckless Dallas (whom Maxwell had sacked in my absence), Patrick, and Dorman. Gavin Boyd himself turned up to give us the full benefit of his advice. We were determined not to be stampeded.

With Maxwell seated beside me to my left, I went over yet again and at some length the reasons for the council's decision. When I had finished Maxwell looked round the table for a friendly face but found none.

He said: "If there's to be no evening edition I shall disassociate myself from the company. I shall resign from the board, from the co-chairmanship and the position of publisher. In fact I shall sever every connection with the company."

Boyd sat apparently unimpressed and then gave his legal opinion. He reminded Maxwell that he had a responsibility as a director to recognise the commitments made in the prospectus. They had not been made lightly and could not be lightly dismissed. If Maxwell wished to change the commitments made when the cash was raised then he had a clear duty to convene a meeting of the shareholders and seek their consent for any changes. "Take care," he warned, "what you are doing."

Maxwell's attitude softened considerably. "All I want to do is to increase our chances of advertising. If we don't get enough advertising we'll be dead in no time."

Dorman intervened. "Are you telling us now, at this stage, that there is a danger of there being a shortfall in advertising revenue, after all your guarantees."

"I do."

Dorman looked at him in apparent astonishment and then slowly shook his head.

I decided to wind up the discussion. There seemed little point in prolonging it since irrespective of the legal arguments the evening paper could not be done technically.

Maxwell stormed: "Then I withdraw my investment."

There was a pause. Dorman was attempting to light his Meerschaum, puffing a cloud of smoke that partly hid his face. Then he said:

"Please, Mr Maxwell, will you please tell us how?"

"I'll just stop the cheque."

"I'm afraid it's too late now. Your cheque was actioned yesterday and there's nothing you can do about it now. Your cash is an investment and cannot be reconverted back to cash."

The legal advisers then left us and Maxwell now cooled down. Indeed he became almost contrite. But the meeting still was going badly for him. His next demand was that since he was the publisher his name ought to appear on the *News* imprint. Our reaction was predictable. Again he withdrew it, sheepishly asking if his name could instead appear on the stationery. We could not even agree to that.

Next he told us of his final arrangements with Dench. By this time we had got completely on top of him and continued with the rout. Dench arrived. He was beginning to show his years; he was by no means the bundle of energy we felt we needed. He told us that he had been appointed advertising director by Maxwell and was free to engage whatever staff he felt necessary and at rates he thought appropriate. These were the terms on which he was taking the job. Armstrong had been fidgeting and now tackled Dench. It was sheer lunacy, he said. No wonder the *Express* had gone to the wall. In this company we were staff and wage conscious. "You will have to live with our philosophy if you intend to stay with us."

Dench looked for support but Maxwell said nothing. Then he said he could not possibly continue his association with the company. It shocked him to learn that the evening edition was not going ahead. "But now when I hear that I am not now to be allowed to determine my own department's staffing and wage levels, I have no alternative but to resign. Your co-operative can never hope to work."

With that he seized his briefcase and left. It was just as well. Earlier in the day we had persuaded Jimmy Galt to take the job. Within 90 minutes he was before the council and appointed advertisement manager. He was to make a success of it; but had he been appointed sooner, had the debate about an evening edition been more quickly resolved, then the advertising department would have been better geared to bringing in revenue. As it was it was mainly Galt's drive and professionalism that carried the paper at first.

The council now pressed home its ascendancy over Maxwell. First Blyth demanded the undated letters of resignation be destroyed. Agreed. Then Maxwell capitulated on the choice of the company's insurers. Then he bounced back. We would be pleased to learn, he said, that he had negotiated the purchase of newsprint for a year from a company that had agreed to cut its price from £165 to £154 a tonne. "Now what do you think of that? That's the sort of business I can do for you."

When we pressed him he refused to name the company. "The deal is a personal one," he said. "If I am not involved it will be called off. I can say no more."

Armstrong pointed out that there was around £2m involved. Russell pressed him to honour the spirit of the co-operative and tell us. Maxwell was beginning to be nettled.

He said: "In the name of God, I know exactly what I am doing. I've explained the circumstances of the contract, the need for secrecy. What else do you all want of me?"

Russell probed further. Maxwell admitted that a Scandinavian company had been in touch with us but had sent a letter calling off their deal. Russell and I read the letter quickly. It implied clearly that Maxwell had been trying to persuade them to buy shares in the company as part of the deal. But they would not accept his conditions. Russell asked: "Whose shares would they have bought? Were you trying to offload some of your own shares and reduce your own risk? If they were not your own shares why did you keep the deal a secret from the members of the council?"

Russell's manner was inoffensive but Maxwell bristled. "They would have been company issues, not mine. You have no right to suggest otherwise."

Russell answered with a smile.

Ten days passed before we secured details of the deal from Charles de Selincourt of British International Press. The cost was £152 per tonne, not £165. Maxwell had ordered 12,000 tonnes, our needs came nearer 9,000. All the supplies were to come from one company, bad practice since it created dependence on a single source. He had ordered the wrong weight of paper which, if run in the presses, would have been torn to shreds. After a lengthy meeting de Selincourt agreed to tear up the contract.

Another point of difference emerged at our meeting. Maxwell protested vociferously when we decided to deposit more than £500,000 in reserves with the City of Glasgow. Our decision had been reached for commercial and social reasons. The city's interest rate was competitive and the withdrawal arrangements suited us. Placing our cash there had an added bonus in the shape of our fair share of advertising: the council would rank among our top advertisers. Socially, we argued that the money should be used to help attract industry to the city. The decision had been well discussed but Maxwell demanded that the money be invested in a commercial bank in London at terms half a point higher. We were suspicious of this arrangement. Despite a heated debate that threatened to descend to the level of personal abuse we stuck to our decision.

On the Friday the tension became explosive. Maxwell took it on himself to give a press statement en route back to Oxford despite an agreement not to do so. He said that an evening paper had been a condition of his investment and he would continue to fight for it in the council. He would hold up the purchase of the building till he had his way. I phoned Dorman and we convened a meeting at 2.30pm.

The time had come to stand up or walk away. We had tried hard to develop a working arrangement with Maxwell, but it was becoming increasingly obvious that Maxwell did not want to work with us. I asked Dorman about the legal position. There were no major difficulties he said, about removing Maxwell's executive powers. But only the shareholders could remove him from the board. He outlined various options, of which one was that we might offer him the post of deputy chairman, non-executive.

McNamara said: "Let's not waste time. Let's chase the bugger back to his big house in Oxford." Armstrong took the cue. He moved that Maxwell be removed from executive authority and as co-chairman. There were no amendments but I still wanted a vote for the records. Only Blyth would not record his vote but when I formally put Armstrong's motion I asked that it should receive unanimous support. To my surprise and relief it was carried unanimously.

ON SATURDAY morning, having procrastinated as long as I could, I forced myself to phone Maxwell in Oxford. But once through to him I felt composed. After all, he had more reason to be nervous than I. I told him that Tony Benn was coming to the building the next day to talk to the council. We were particularly anxious that he be present because we wanted to define his responsibilities.

"Excellent, Allister, excellent," he replied. "We cannot continue in the present muddle."

The conversation wasn't going as planned. Oh well, in at the deep end:

"You see, we have decided unanimously to sack you as an executive director and, further, to remove you as co-chairman."

I can't recall the full text of his comments but they were not scripted to flatter me. At one stage he said: "You've conned me, you've conned me." And in a broad sense I suppose he was right. Tough stood at my side, thumbs up and grinning broadly. At last the council had confronted and surmounted its chief obstacle – Robert Maxwell.

That evening I received a phone call at home. Maxwell's ill-humour had by now softened, and it was a reasoning and persuasive voice that addressed me. We went over the issues between us.

He said: "On your own, without my guidance, you will make mistakes."

"None so monumental as yours, I assure you."

He then conceded that really his behaviour had been inexcusable "but only because I'm so anxious for us to make a success of the company."

He continued: "Make this offer to the lads – I shall relinquish my executive authority but am anxious to remain as co-chairman. You understand that the office means nothing to me. But it would have a bad publicity effect on the paper and a demoralising effect on the workforce if I were to be removed from the post."

His offer did not seem likely to be accepted but nonetheless I agreed to make it on his behalf. At the meeting, which was held on late Sunday morning, I recapitulated Friday's decision. Maxwell hung on every word, nodding his head slowly. He confessed that his behaviour had been "inexcusable" but it had been from the best of motives. It was true that he had told the management to report to him directly. "I made a mistake there." Of course, they should be answerable to the council. The title of co-chairman meant nothing to him but he pointed out that it had been a condition of his investment. He had insisted that he be responsible for the commercial and financial decisions of the company and that Mackie should look after staffing and so on. "All of you agreed."

Armstrong's eyes bulged with dislike. "Of course we agreed," he broke in. "What else could we have done? You were blackmailing us at the time. But you won't blackmail us now."

After further discussion, during which he apologised for trying to sack Tough, I said: "The mistake you made was that you believed you could intimidate us. You were wrong there. You cannot threaten an unemployed man. There is nothing you can take from him."

Maxwell rose and said in a quiet voice: "Allister, will you now put to the council the proposals I put to you last night over the phone." He left the room. My head was in a turmoil as I tried to recall the offer. But Blyth spoke. He moved that we invite Maxwell to continue as co-chairman but in a non-executive capacity.

That, indeed, was Maxwell's offer. Had he phoned Blyth? No, was the reply. But, said Blyth, we were just ordinary workers. I (Mackie) was just a compositor. What could I know about running a business? We needed Maxwell's experience in business. In the argument that followed Blyth persisted. We needed Maxwell, or somebody like him, capable of making the correct commercial decisions. He received support from neither members nor advisers. The discussion was still in progress when Maxwell came in again.

"Have you reached a decision?" he demanded.

I told him the council was still resolved that he should be removed both from the co-chairmanship and his executive role.

"In that case," he said, "I demand the right to appeal directly to the members at a mass meeting."

I demurred but Blyth supported Maxwell who, he said, as a member of the co-operative must be allowed to address the members.

"That man," I reminded the meeting, "is not a member of the co-operative. He is not an employee, therefore not a member. It is true that he has asked for employee shares but we have refused them. If we decide to allow him to address a mass meeting and to appeal to it, then it will not be as a right, but as a privilege. Understand that point clearly."

Flushed with our successful handling of Maxwell, the council agreed to allow him to appeal direct to the membership of the co-operative provided there was no leak to the workforce of the council's decision. Thus was the seed sown that would destroy the co-operative and our dreams of workforce control.

CHAPTER TWELVE

Bombshell from Benn

WHEN TONY BENN arrived I told him that we had bombed out Maxwell as co-chairman and as executive director. He gave a non-committal nod and said, "Good luck". To the members of the co-operative he stood for everything that was worthwhile in the world of politics. We believed he was mainly responsible for the Government support; he had stood by us when the cynics and pessimists had sought to destroy us. But for him and his few supporters in government the battle would have been lost long ago. In his address to members, assembled on the editorial floor, he applauded our tenacity, fighting spirit and faith in the co-operative principle.

Afterwards Benn met us in the room we were using as our headquarters. It was not large, and mostly taken up with a large wooden table. All the seats round the table were quickly occupied. We had decided to invite all the original members of the Action Committee and those members of management already appointed. There were probably more people standing than seated.

While I was still trying to bring some order to proceedings, Maxwell started speaking as if on our behalf. He described the writers Sillitto had engaged, the technical problems we had overcome. It was a fantastic piece of impudence. It was as if our previous meeting had never taken place.

Benn surprised me in his short speech. He congratulated us. Then he dropped a bombshell. "Of course," he said, "much must be credited to Mr Maxwell's involvement. His business experience no doubt has guided your decisions in the past and will be of great value to you in the future."

In the months ahead Maxwell was to use the tribute as a weapon with which to attack us. At the time he seemed to swell in importance, not only to himself but to the editorial and management members. I can think of no rational explanation for Benn's slip. I cannot believe he intended the effect that came from it. Perhaps he was merely being courteous.

A general discussion followed during which Macgee made it clear that he was unhappy about Sillitto's views on content. He then hinted at criticism of the council. Once the meeting was over I approached him and reminded him that he was an executive, with a responsibility to support the editor in public and the decisions of the council. He would be entitled to criticise Fred and the council in public only if he resigned as an executive. I walked off. Behind me I could hear him shrieking at my retreating back, threatening to have me before his chapel committee. It had been a bad day.

THE NEXT three days were taken up with preparations for the showdown with Maxwell. The mass meeting had been arranged for the Thursday. On Tuesday afternoon we briefed the FoCs. They looked relieved as they pledged their full support unanimously. On Wednesday the full-time union officials did the same.

By Thursday morning the tension was at boiling point. At the council meeting that preceded the mass meeting, Maxwell again tried to change our resolve. Blyth again supported the compromise. We all sat quietly round the table but our decision was final.

Within minutes we were walking through to the editorial floor. I confess I was filled with uncertainty. Maxwell had been canvassing the editorial department. We heard reports that Macgee and most of the others had pledged him their support. If their oratory won the day I knew I would resign immediately and set about the break-up of the enterprise. There was for me no acceptable alternative. My intentions had never been discussed with the others but I knew that they would join me if it came to the bit.

Every little detail of Maxwell's behaviour since we had raised the cash was explained to the workforce. The grapevine had kept them well informed. But they did seem genuinely surprised by the extent of his interference. I was never abusive about Maxwell but he launched into a vitriolic personal attack on me and the other councillors with the exception of Blyth. The accusations were wild and erratic. This was a street brawler, not a debater. What surprised me most was his complete lack of judgment. As he spoke the workforce became more and more hostile. Then it boiled over when he made his biggest gaffe.

"I assure you, brothers, there was no trouble between the council members and myself until Mr Bighead Mackie came back from Paris."

The howl of protest drowned the rest of his sentence.

Goldberg was one of the first to speak from the shop floor. He criticised not Maxwell but the councillors for having discussed the Maxwell sacking with the FoCs and full-time officials before they had informed the workforce. He spoke on Maxwell's behalf saying that we were now living in a jungle and that we needed someone with Maxwell's animal instincts to help us. He wound up: "Bob will just have to behave himself, and to live with the other members of the council." He moved that his executive authority be removed but that he remain as co-chairman. He would not be allowed to negotiate deals or sign cheques. "That should remove all of the councillors' fears of him."

Macgee seconded the motion and thus seemed to confirm a Blyth/Goldberg/Macgee collusion. Briston tried to quote from the Department of Trade report on Maxwell's performance at Pergamon. But he was howled down by Goldberg, Macgee and other journalists.

Maxwell leapt to his feet and, face distorted with rage, stabbed a forefinger at Briston and bawled: "I'll issue a writ against you. Briston, you won't get away with this!"

Without Briston's help none of us would have been there. For his reward he had been howled down by a mindless pack. It was a sad moment. But conscience and truth were to be the first casualties in the struggle for control. As the meeting went on it was evident the workforce were determined to remove Maxwell – but were reluctant to go the whole road. Goldberg, as they saw it, offered a compromise.

Maxwell, smelling victory, demanded a ballot vote. Backed by Dorman, I immediately ruled him out of order. I proposed a 30-minute adjournment. As we trooped back into the council room hardly a word was exchanged. Predictably Blyth was the first to support the compromise. Others followed. Sillitto produced a draft press release. It said that the Works Council had decided that "Mr Robert Maxwell, co-chairman of the *Scottish Daily News*, has today relinquished executive authority in the affairs of the company, and will be working jointly with the council to achieve the successful early launch and subsequent viability of the enterprise." Maxwell tried to prevent any press release going out at all but eventually we all agreed to it.

Back at the meeting I had almost finished reading it when Maxwell jumped to his feet and demanded there should be no press release. By this time the workforce could stomach no more of his tactics and roughly told him to sit down and shut up. Thus ended his first grab for control. We had won and Maxwell knew it.

Armstrong and I were at the main door later on in the afternoon as Maxwell was entering a taxi to be driven to Glasgow Airport. He was the picture of a defeated man as he sat slumped in the seat. His face was a mask of dejection, his muscles were slack and the sparkle had gone from his manner. I think I felt sorry for him but I was strengthened at the same time, because I had won a vital battle and now knew that Maxwell could feel pain. There would be other battles, because he would keep coming back, but we had taken him on and thrashed him. That was the last I saw of him until the day the paper was launched.

THE PREPARATORY work resumed with fresh enthusiasm. We would gather all the heads of department together to discuss every problem they encountered. They learned to appreciate and understand each other's difficulties. On April 28 a dummy run was organised. We reviewed our problems. Weaknesses were unearthed. But the biggest surprise came when we counted the number of man hours required to sheet up the machines. In the Beaverbrook days more than 100 hours were being allowed. We were doing the operation in five hours and every bit as efficiently! The cycle of dummy runs continued: produce and criticise, produce and criticise. Our progress was phenomenal. By the Friday night our problems all seemed to have been overcome. By this weekend our members had received their first wage for more than a year – and they had earned every penny of it. No-one worked to the clock. The chapels offered suggestions to improve production and redeploy members to where they were most needed.

With every successful dummy run spirits and expectations rose higher. Some of the engineers, facing bigger problems than other departments, were working 14 hours a day. Willie Clarke, their chief, took to sleeping in his office. There was no Maxwell to foul up our progress.

During this period McNamara and Armstrong made a TV appearance they had cause to regret later. A *World In Action* team were filming our preparations. They asked to be allowed to record a meeting of council members and the editor. There were four of us at the meeting – Sillitto, McNamara, Armstrong and myself. I warned the pair to be cautious but as the meeting progressed they seemed intoxicated by the excitement. At the time we were studying one of the dummy papers which contained articles by Teddy Taylor, the Conservative MP, and other articles of doubtful political complexion. McNamara and Armstrong attacked Sillitto in a way I had never seen before. It was vicious, giving the viewer the impression that Sillitto was being bullied into selecting contents reflecting only a narrow political outlook. The entire performance was artificial and out of character and the producer exaggerated the effect by cuts and angles. It was to be thrown in their face by editorial members, almost on the day the *News* finally folded, as a major reason for its poor sales performance.

During this period also Russell and I went through the business of buying the building. The scene took place in Beaverbrook's Glasgow lawyers' office. Russell, Patrick and I, together with other laywers, were joined by a small dapper man with a weather-beaten face and a goatee beard. He looked for all the world like a retired sea-captain. He introduced himself as an official from the Treasury. Patrick presented him with certificates showing we had raised the £1.2m required of us. He scrutinised them and then went into an adjoining room to call his departmental heads in London.

Within three minutes he was back with the news that "it" had been done.

"What's been done?" I asked.

"The Treasury at this moment are depositing the first payment of their loan into your account in London. That is what has been done."

I felt a glow. There was no Maxwell to spoil the occasion, for once. Within a couple of minutes our balance had been reduced by £850,000. Russell and I signed a cheque payable to Beaverbrook for the purchase of the building. That morning I had signed on at the dole. I was unemployed and totally broke, I reflected as I signed it. It was a strange world.

Now we waited for Sunday evening. For more than 13 months we had fought for that day. Dreams and hope had sustained us. We had crawled and scratched our way forward. We were standing on the edge of the promised land. We couldn't know what it held in store but we were impatient to find out.

PART TWO
The birth and death

CHAPTER THIRTEEN

A sense of betrayal

May 4, 1975

THE MORNING of our launch came at last. Months before I had committed myself to speak at a seminar organised by the British Institute of Management, and by chance it fell on this day. I rose at 5.30 and drove, on a warm and sunny morning, the 150 miles to Aviemore. The trip on empty roads gave me a chance to collect myself. Events had piled on events. We had been given precious little time to pause; yet that was what we most needed to do.

The run-up from a technical point of view had been an unqualified, indeed a fantastic, success. But the circumstances had exposed one fundamental problem, and it involved Tough. As chairman I had directed the operation but undoubtedly the success had been due to the co-operative involvement of the heads of department and the FoCs. But Tough ought to have been directing the show, not I. He was general manager but unfortunately knew nothing of the techniques of producing a newspaper. And so, although it was against my repeatedly stated principles of divorcing the executive and management functions, I was forced, in the interests of the production of the paper, to cross the line. Again, when we were negotiating the purchase of the newsprint the executive council, by sheer weight of necessity, had had to step into a management function. There had been other times when we had had to swallow our ideals to make sure the job was done correctly. I also had doubts about Tough's ability to survive in the hurly-burly of the co-operative. Were his management skills more theoretical than practical? After all, his previous experience had been as a consultant. And could he control the editorial and put

145

backbone into Sillitto? Finally I suspected that his politics were those of a Right-wing Conservative and that he might harbour contempt for the whole co-operative principle.

By dinnertime I was driving south again. Back in Bathgate I picked up my wife and headed for Albion Street, where the excitement was bubbling. There I met Tom Band of the DTI who gave me the last-minute arrangements for meeting Tony Benn. Band, my wife and I drove to Glasgow Airport to meet him. We were the only people, said Band, who knew he was coming, apart from a few airport officials. With Mrs Benn he arrived in a light aircraft and on the way back to Glasgow he asked me about Maxwell.

"Do you think you've sorted him out this time?" he asked. "Have you any fears there?"

I replied that, yes, he was still there and would stay there as long as he had money involved. "It's a pity we couldn't just buy him out. Give him his money and chase him back to Oxford and let us get on with our paper."

It was a pity, Benn agreed. But the Government's loan was conditional on his investment. "I doubt if anything can be done about it now. You'll have to sort out the problem the best way you can in the circumstances. Your lads have shown a remarkable resilience up to now. I think they'll keep him in check." I did not share his confidence. We had not succeeded in educating our members on the philosophy of the co-operative. We had even failed to convince the entire Action Committee.

When we arrived at Albion Street I felt sick to the pit of my stomach. Maxwell was standing, hands outstretched, as if welcoming Benn into his own household. Before long we were posing for photographs – the three of us with Maxwell's arms entwined with ours. The *News* photographer wanted to take pictures of Maxwell and Benn, excluding me. It was an indication of editorial thinking but with an angry word in his ear I soon re-adjusted his priorities.

Benn and his wife could not wait for the launch but asked for a conducted tour. By this time the party had been joined by Gregor Mackenzie in his capacity as a Treasury Minister. I knew every corner of the building and the function of almost every piece of equipment and I felt able to take them round without the assistance of Jimmy Roy, the production manager, who was heavily engaged getting things ready in the machine room. Maxwell insisted on coming with us and no sooner had we left the boardroom than he took over. I tried to regain control of the tour but short of having an all-out battle with him there was little I could do. Benn recognised the situation and tried to detach himself from Maxwell but even with all his tact and experience he could not evade his leech-like attentions. As we entered the machine-room Mackenzie could take no more and whispered to me: "You lads will have to do something here. That man believes the paper is his. You must remember that the loan was made on the understanding that this was a co-operative . . . Live up to your responsibilities." There was no need for the homily but the situation, as he must have seen it, was that the Government had made a loan of £1.2m to help Maxwell set up a newspaper.

Benn and his wife left shortly afterwards. In the street outside a pipe band played while in the board room an invited party gathered – supporters and celebrities, business friends, civic and church leaders. Among them was Kathleen McCafferty, a student teacher at Jordanhill College. We had selected her to push the button to set the presses rolling. On the morning we had launched the prospectus she had come to the Hut to make an investment. Only Armstrong and I were there at around nine on a wild bleak morning of sleet. We had been sitting full of doubt about the public response and the arrival of this charming, dark-haired, blue-eyed young lady had been a tonic. She had borrowed money from her mother to make up her £25.

Soon word came from the caseroom that the last page was almost ready to be moulded. It had been decided that since I had locked up the last page of the *Scottish Daily Express* I should finish off the final page of the first edition of the *News*. Fraser Ross was at the head of the page, his hands and forearms as ever stained with ink, and Stewart Murdoch at the bottom. I felt a bit self-conscious as I went through the motions of finishing their work. The page was passed by Alec Munro, the head printer, as being in good typographical condition, but even now Maxwell tried to get into the act by taking over from Murdoch. But Murdoch had been warned and was just that bit more determined to share in the moment.

A vast cheer rose. The official party made its way down to the machine-room where the TV cameras were waiting. The lights were dazzling as I made my way to the centre of the scene only to find that

147

Maxwell was there before me. He had carefully placed himself in the best position for the cameras. Kathleen was given a temporary union card, the plates were locked, the register was checked. Kathleen made a short speech and pushed the button. The klaxon sounded and then the presses were running. It was a great moment but for me it lacked the personal delight I had experienced in the caseroom.

Out in the street the blue-liveried vans set out into the night with their loads of hope. Then I rejoined the celebrations. As I climbed the stairs to the fourth floor I was surprised to hear the strains of *The Red Flag* coming from the old boardroom. There was Matt McGinn, a well-known Glasgow folk singer, leading the singing, surrounded by various "politicals". On the wall behind there was an oblong-shaped mark where in the old days the portrait of Lord Beaverbrook had hung in what had then been the holy of holies. Times had changed.

The paper proved a disappointment. Once all the brouhaha had died down and I had the chance to take a good look at it, I felt a sense that somehow I had been betrayed. The front-page lead was trivial, and this in the first issue of a radical new newspaper that was going to add a new dimension to the industry. I discussed it with no-one, preferring to save my comments for a more appropriate time. As it happened, almost all the councillors had been harbouring the same feelings. Russell and Armstrong were waiting for me at the office in the morning. Russell's verdict was bleak: our paper was rubbish. There had been lots of good news stories in the other papers; we had missed out on at least half of them. The lead was of a young girl who had "died" but had been brought back to life. The heading ran, "It's good to be alive!"

We climbed the stairs to the fourth floor. In the council room we were joined by McNamara (the other councillors at this time were on night shift). Almost word for word he repeated the criticisms. I thought he must have discussed the matter with the others but this turned out not to be the case. Russell said he had raised it with Sillitto but had been told that the choice of news had been made specifically to attract readers: they had not wanted to go in with a heavy news coverage on the first edition. None of us could follow the line of reasoning but accepted the assurances that there would be an improvement from now on. All of us felt deeply uneasy.

THE FOLLOWING three weeks passed so quickly that none of us had time to catch our breath. Formal council meetings went by the board while Tough was left with the responsibility of getting the paper out. The early days showed little if any improvement in the standard of journalism. Some of the pages were so bad that I was embarrassed to be recognised as being involved with the *News*. Within days of the launch I had to appear at a seminar in London. At Edinburgh Airport I bought my *News* and had a quick glance through it. The contents were pathetic. By the time we were airborne I had hidden my paper away and was hoping that no-one would recognise me. The front-page lead told the story of a young boy who had had his toy car stolen by young thieves, and how the *News* had bought him a new toy. In the inside pages were trite articles by writers whose messages were either too clever for me to comprehend or were just plain rubbish – and I suspected the latter.

The fault was undoubtedly Sillitto's. He was unable to exert authority over his editorial staff and at the same time they lacked the skills their positions demanded. In the early days before the launch he had complained to the Works Council that some of his executives, but mainly Macgee, had been undermining his authority. Armstrong, Russell, McNamara and I were unanimous in our advice. We told him to sack Macgee: that would be a lesson to the others. If he was not prepared to do that himself, he should make an official complaint to us and we would do it for him. He did neither. Macgee was, on the contrary, made assistant editor, though only after a drama. Sillitto decided to appoint Goldberg as his deputy. Macgee got wind of it and created such a fuss about it that Goldberg went to the council with the request not to be appointed. Instead he asked Sillitto and the council simply to appoint two assistant editors, Macgee and himself: he would take the responsibilities of deputy editor with Macgee taking charge of the day-shift journalistic work. As it turned out, Macgee proved a success in the role but his hold over Sillitto and the other journalists was frightening. Sillitto was too gentle for his job, taking refuge in the leader column. He learned the lesson that authority, if not exercised, is soon lost. Before long the journalists were engaged in squabbles among themselves on matters like content and political attitudes, which in reality should have been decided by the editor with no more than basic guidance from the Works Council. More and more the editor cocooned himself in a shell of trivia until near anarchy reigned. Decisions went to the loudest voice, invariably that of Goldberg or Macgee.

My mornings at this period always began with an informal chat with Tough, then a full session with members of the management team. Tough chaired these meetings since they were part of his management functions. One morning before the management meeting we discussed a football report in the paper which Tough had found inadequate. I had read it too and thought it poorly written, lacking professionalism. The public, without being fully aware of what was wrong, would realise something was missing and in time would stop buying the paper.

I said: "If we get rid of most of our editorial executives and replace them with people who know what they are doing, then we stand a chance. What I should like us to do is contact Mary Holland of the *Observer*. I know she is sympathetic to us and has the talent to have a go at making the paper worthwhile. We can make her deputy editor immediately, if she's willing, we'll promote her to editor after she has found her feet. Let's discuss it with Fred."

Tough was happy with the suggestion. Sillitto, as I had expected, proved amenable. He accepted there was a fundamental problem to be sorted out and that it could not be left to the existing journalists. In time some might mature but they were not ready yet. He was painfully aware of his own shortcomings.

But how could we protect her from the hostility that I knew would come from the other editorial executives? On my insistence the approach to her would be kept secret: otherwise they would destroy her.

She was contacted. Sillitto and I met her at Glasgow Airport and lunched with her in the restaurant there. She is a charming person, feminine to her fingertips despite her successes in what is very much a man's world. Her professional expertise was enormous. When she heard of what we wanted of her she was enthusiastic: she would love to be part of it. I felt elated – here was the answer to our worries. Soon we were discussing what arrangements should be made to have her family accommodated and how to go about looking for a house for her. But she insisted that she visit the office right away so that she could absorb more of the spirit of the workforce. I hesitated. This was the part I feared. But how could I put my fears into words without frightening her off? She picked up my hesitancy.

"Is there some reason why I shouldn't go?" she asked.

Sillitto came to my rescue. "Allister is afraid of my executives," he said. "He thinks they will try to peck you to death rather than risk allowing you to be put in a position to judge them. He is entirely wrong of course."

The explanation was dismissed with a delicate movement of her hand. "I assure you I live in a man's world and I have learned how to look after myself. Don't worry over me for a second."

But I did. In no way could she alone tackle experienced agitators like Macgee. They would stamp on her as on a butterfly. And they did. After a brief, friendly meeting with the members of the council, Sillitto introduced her to his executives. I do not know for sure what took place in the confines of the editor's office. Reports were given to me of a severe grilling and hostility open and bitter. I do know that as she entered the editorial department she was greeted by a semi-drunken journalist who greeted her with, "So you're Mary Holland who writes about Northern Ireland. Well I'll let you know we are Orangemen in here and don't need your sort."

The journalist was not typical but he did indicate the feeling that had been building up ever since news of her interest had percolated out during the day.

She never started. Very politely and discreetly she bowed out of her commitment. It had been unfair to ask her in the first place. The episode was just the death of another hope.

CHAPTER FOURTEEN

Clouds of suspicion

THE PAPER slowly started its death throes. On the first night there was a sell-out with 250,000 copies sold. The second day's sale reached 317,000, the third about 330,000. From that day the decline set in. During the second week sales were falling by as much as 20,000 a day. By the end of the week they had slumped to 200,000. Yet the editorial content did not even then improve. We could not conceal from ourselves the truth that we were producing a bad newspaper. There were no production problems. The members' enthusiasm had to be seen to be believed: it was total commitment and their end product was possibly one of the best produced newspapers in the country. But it was not enough and Eric Tough was seriously worried. If the trend continued the paper would die in a few weeks while there was still plenty of cash in the bank. He aired his fears at an unofficial get-together between some members of the council and editorial executives. Macgee was first to offer an explanation for the developing crisis. It had been brought about, he said, by the bad impression created by Charlie Armstrong and Jimmy McNamara in the *World in Action* programme. "The public," he said, "now believes that our paper is controlled by extremists who bully our editor and determine the paper's contents."

The suggestion was preposterous but understandable. They could not possibly accept that they were the cause of the problem. Removing Armstrong and McNamara was an easier solution and a less painful one than replacing the editorial executives. Tough shook his head in disbelief. The responsibility lay with editorial. If the public wouldn't buy the paper then it could only be because they did not believe it was good enough. But it became evident at this meeting that the editorial executives would not be able to accept that their own lack of ability was the root cause of the paper's problems. Now the paper was not all bad. Some of the work by the journalists was top-class. A campaign was launched to re-open the case of Paddy Meehan, convicted for murder (and later pardoned). There was a successful campaign to save steelworkers' jobs in Lanarkshire. A betting group was exposed for sacking trade unionists. But there just wasn't enough talent to go round. There was also a lack of maturity and balance.

AFTER THE launch I had decided to return to work in the caseroom as a compositor. But it didn't work out like that. There was too much to do. After a week I returned to take up my duties as full-time company chairman. Life was more comfortable in the caseroom but as long as I was not in occupation in the council room there was the danger that Maxwell might appear to fill the vacuum. Maxwell was absent in body but not in spirit. When we gave a presentation to advertisers in London, hostile stories about the commercial performance of the *News* appeared in the *Daily Telegraph*. We were disturbed to learn from a *Guardian* reporter that Maxwell had phoned his office to give a distorted picture of the state of the *News*. As it turned out our presentation in London was well attended. Tremendous interest was shown but little hard business followed.

Meanwhile Roy Patrick, our lawyer, was briefing me for the first general meeting. I had tried to have this postponed but he told me that though we had been operating as a newspaper only for a short spell the company had been formed for a year and the meeting was demanded by the Companies Act. The method of electing the directors was for a first vote to be taken as a vote of confidence in all of them. If all were thus endorsed there would be no election. That seemed to me the best way of ensuring the return of Armstrong and McNamara, the only councillors where there seemed to be doubt. Many of the workforce were being persuaded by the journalists that the cause of the paper's falling circulation had been their performance on *World in Action*. Meanwhile Maxwell, operating from London, was attempting to undermine the council's authority. He relied on the support of the editorial executives, who also controlled the editorial chapel, and the caseroom malcontents (and there always had been more than enough of them). On the evening of May 20 he sent every works councillor and FoC a telex 8ft long. It reminded us that his involvement was at the invitation of ourselves – and Tony Benn. He predicted disaster for the paper unless he was recalled to run it. McNamara and Armstrong were criticised for their performance on *World in Action* (which pointed to collusion between Maxwell and the journalists). It was full of inaccuracies about sales figures, running costs and anything that might make the situation look worse. He ended by claiming that his assessment had been made according to figures supplied to him by Tough. This Tough denied and argued that in fact the position was far from desperate.

The reaction of the FoCs was to convene a meeting, listen to our report, then pass a vote objecting to Maxwell's interference. But Maxwell had achieved the desired effect. The Works Council was doing badly, was behaving badly in public and had no solution to the co-operative's problems. No vote could erase the workforce's fears and bolster their sagging confidence.

The few meetings held by the council had become increasingly difficult. Suspicion clouded the air. Blyth was now isolated from us. We suspected he was in contact with Maxwell and the journalists and we held unofficial meetings without him so we could have discussions in depth. At one of them Armstrong suggested that we should all stand or fall together. If any one of us was put off the council, the others would resign along with that member. Russell and I disagreed with him and the idea was dropped. Such a step could have led to Maxwell's complete control at a stroke. The only way he could be held at bay was by canvassing against him. Already the FoCs had promised unanimous support to the sitting councillors. But George Welsh, the editorial FoC, had not attended the meeting. Joe McGowan of the caseroom, in casting his vote, admitted that he could not guarantee that he was speaking for the majority of his members. This lack of support by both departments was a constant stab in the back. It proved to be the power-base from which Maxwell worked.

It seemed to me that the caseroom attitude was a natural progression from their age-old mistrust of the other chapels in the building. Somehow they seemed to identify the Works Council as a natural successor to the Federated Chapel of the Beaverbrook days and they had consistently threatened to quit that body. Their collective attitude had always been one of standing apart from the other chapels. They were not happy to be identified with them, in particular the non-craft unions. Their attitude seemed somehow related to their union's consistent decision not to have a political affiliation.

I had observed during the *Express* days their sensitivity to wage differentials between them and non-craft unions. Once when Beaverbrook had as usual pleaded poverty, they had discussed accepting a wage cut – provided that the unskilled Natsopa members accepted the same reduction, thus widening percentage differentials between the two groups. Often caseroom demands for wages were related more to the question of differentials than to the cash itself. Some members of other chapels used to remark cynically that the caseroom was populated with masons and Orangemen. I never found this to be an accurate comment. When I had first joined the *Express* the masonic influence had been a power to worry about. But for a few years before the closure of the *Express* there had been less of a tendency for the masons, and there were still many of them, to act as a group. In fact they ceased to consider themselves a people apart. Roman Catholics and non-masonic people held as much influence as the dwindling masonic population. This had been a welcome development which had broken down the mistrust and hostility that for too long had perverted the relationships among compositors. The masonic phenomenon was true not just of the *Express*. It obtained in the printing industry, certainly in the west of Scotland. When I was an apprentice in Kilmarnock there were then around 56 members in our branch. The area covered from Darvel to Irvine. In all of that membership, to my certain knowledge, there was only one Roman Catholic, Michael Murphy. He taught me my apprenticeship in a small local newspaper in Kilmarnock and was, despite his uniqueness, the union branch president. The anti-Catholic bias there did not come from the employees – it was a gentlemen's agreement among the employers. Nor was this an exclusively caseroom phenomenon. I remember the occasion when an FoC of the Natsopa chapel boasted that he had beaten the masonic dominance by an unlikely coalition of Labour Party supporters, communists and Catholics!

Now the compositors were beginning to ally themselves to the editorial chapel which had in the *Express* days always had an elitist outlook. The journalists seemed to see the tradesmen and the general workers not as partners but as an encumbrance necessary for the production of their newspapers. They were the real creators – the professionals. The contributions of others required less talent; therefore they had to be tolerated. They had been full members of the old Federated House Chapel but when it came to the essentials they had always taken their own course. The Beaverbrook management had encouraged this division, with separate pension, sick-scheme and other arrangements. Perhaps it was this elitist outlook of the so-called professional class that prevented their complete integration. In the days of the Action Committee they resented the fact that electricians, engineers, clerical workers and others were able to make decisions that would affect them and their working conditions.

The editor's inability to control them worsened the situation. They claimed full expenses as if they had forgotten that the Beaverbrook organisation had pulled stumps. Most, though not all, claimed every penny to which they were entitled. In some cases Tough and I unearthed claims that had no justification at all. Tough was also incensed by their claims that articles written outside their normal duties should be paid. His observations were unheeded. The foreign sub-editor was being paid more than £34 a week for his daily contribution of foreign snippets, a task that should have been no more than a labour of love. The sports editor was claiming extra for his darts column, which Tough and I refused to agree to. As a consequence I received a letter from the journalists' FoC, George Welsh, complaining about our decision whereas other executives had already been paid for articles written in their spare time. It was a sad letter to receive. Engineers had been working, some for 14-hour shifts, with no extra payment, to get the paper going. Compositors, clerical workers, everyone had been making contributions that were beyond their normal duties. In addition we had preached to everyone the need to conserve every penny, to be as mean as possible when parting with cash. Cash was the life-blood of the company: without it there was nothing. I grudged every halfpenny with which I was forced to part.

As a matter of course I attended meetings of the FoCs. At one it was suggested that a report of Maxwell's involvement be prepared and distributed to the workforce. In the discussion that followed McGowan of the caseroom chapel said his members had been kept informed of everything but if they chose not to believe it there was nothing in the world that could persuade them. "A lot of our lads couldn't care less about a co-operative," he said. "All they want is a job. And they would work for the devil for their wages if it was necessary, let alone Maxwell. Some among them are even arguing that it will take someone like Maxwell to sort out the journalists."

The decision was taken to have the statement issued. It was left to me to do it on behalf of the Works Council. The following day I circulated it. In it I listed some of the proposals that had been put by Maxwell – delay the launch for a month while putting the staff on full wages (which would have caused an oncost of £100,000); scrub the daily and produce an evening only; restrict circulation to the West of Scotland; introduce a 24-hour paper from the start even though there was not enough staff to produce it. The report concluded that any one of these ideas if implemented would have put the paper in serious trouble and a combination of any two could have killed it.

It had been our hope that the statement would open a grand debate. It was intended not as an attack on Maxwell's character but as a vindication of our actions. It did little to help us. It was treated with scepticism in the editorial and the caseroom. Tough, to back up the principles of workforce involvement, issued a statement, in confidence, setting out the trading position in full. It was a remarkable document and it is unlikely that any other workforce could have been so well informed.

But everything hinged on the outcome of the general meeting, arranged for June 4. Those of us who opposed Maxwell intended to push for the re-election of the existing councillors, including Blyth. Our decision to support Blyth seems strange in retrospect. Our hope was to keep the workforce totally united against Maxwell.

CHAPTER FIFTEEN

Phoney baloney

June 4

A MEETING of the Works Council was held in the morning to go over the agenda and ensure that the General Meeting's business was transacted without a hitch. Briston, Dorman and Patrick attended, as did Tom Band of the DTI "to make sure that everything was above board". Maxwell arrived early and was waiting for us. He started off by making some innocuous remarks about the paper and which evoked a sullen response from Armstrong. Smarting at the rebuff, Maxwell goaded Armstrong. "Come now, Charlie, tell me what you don't like about me. Let all of us know," he invited, embracing the others with a wave of his hand.

"You wouldn't like my reply, Mr Maxwell."

"Come now, Charlie," he persisted. "We are all anxious to know."

Armstrong looked at me. I unleashed him with a silent suggestion of a nod.

"I don't like you, Mr Maxwell, because you are a fucking bastard."

Maxwell's mouth dropped open and he appealed to me. "You now have an answer to your question. Let's get on with the meeting," I said gruffly.

He then launched into an attack on the mismanagement of the company by Tough. He pointed to falling sales but made no reference to the obvious cause of the falling circulation, but did not really make a frontal attack. It was worse. "I don't really blame Eric," he said at one point. "But we all know that he has no experience in newspapers; it's not really his fault." I interrupted to ask what experience he (Maxwell) had of newspapers. He mumbled that he had at one time worked on a German newspaper but I couldn't catch the name.

"Anyway," he continued, "in view of the situation we are in, with all the fighting and mistrust, and because of it, the failing economic situation, I feel I have no alternative but to resign from the council and the co-chairmanship of the company."

Russell looked at him through his glasses. Was he really asking us to believe that he would not seek re-election?

Maxwell tapped him on the knee. "Jimmy," he pleaded, "why must I spell everything out to you? You never seem to trust me. Why?"

Russell replied: "I don't believe for one second that you intend to give up anything. This is no more than another tactic as far as you are concerned. You will never resign so long as there is something in it for you. And you have money invested in the paper."

"We'll wait and see what the members think, the people who really count. We'll see what they say about it." By now Maxwell was mounting a dark fury.

Before the General Meeting could go ahead on the editorial floor, voting slips had to be handed to each employee – only employees would be allowed to vote. Maxwell demanded a voting paper. The teller, a young clerkess, protested that he was not on her list but she allowed him to overwhelm her and eventually she handed over the paper, though still protesting. From the top table Russell and I watched but I suppressed my instinct to walk over and take the paper from him. Russell agreed that he wanted us to fight him on this issue. But if we did it would confuse the membership on the bigger problems.

At the top table Maxwell sat on my left, with Tough on my right. Briston was there to give financial advice if and when it was needed. Patrick and Dorman sat nearby to keep me right on the constitutional side of the business. I explained the voting procedures to the meeting but Maxwell leapt to his feet immediately.

"Fellow co-operators," he said. "This is your company. Don't allow yourselves to be bullied by Mackie and his legal friends. He is talking nonsense. There is no voting procedure laid down by the Companies Act, and even if there was you could afford to forget it.

You are trade unionists, we are all trade unionists together. Let us decide in a democratic manner how we are going to vote. We mustn't allow ourselves to be bullied by Mackie and his fellow councillors. How you must do it is to write down just now, right away, who you wish to sit on the council." With that he started to fill in his own paper.

Goldberg, Macgee, Welsh and other journalists shouted their support, waving their voting papers and creating an atmosphere of total confusion. Armstrong, standing behind me, said in a whisper loud enough for Maxwell to hear. "For the first time since the paper started these bastards have organised themselves well."

After much table-thumping I restored a reasonable amount of calm. I asked Dorman to explain the correct procedures. He rose in an atmosphere of hushed expectancy but before he could speak Maxwell was back on his feet.

"I repeat, this is our company. We don't need advice from these people. We can decide these things for ourselves."

This time there was a hostile reaction. They had learned to trust Dorman and wanted to hear what he had to say. Any other form of voting procedure, he told them, would make the elections null and void. They could well be legally challengeable.

Despite further hostile snortings from Maxwell, Dorman's ruling was accepted without further discussion.

Macgee now took the floor, brushing his mop of white hair from his brow. He referred to the circulation figures and to my introduction in which I had said the paper was not sufficiently attractive to hold readers.

"This is untrue," he said, "and I am astonished to hear you say it." He paused, his head cocked to hear the murmurings of approval from his editorial colleagues.

"I am disappointed that you did not refer to the real cause of the falling sales, which you must surely be aware of."

I knew then what was coming – an assassination attempt on Armstrong and McNamara. "There is the cause at the top table," he went on, pointing to his former Action Committee colleagues. "Their performance in the *World in Action* programme was and remains a disgrace to this co-operative. They have created a public image for the paper which is now surely destroying us."

By this time he was reaching a hysterical crescendo. It was a most impressive performance, so good that I almost forgot that he had never seen the programme.

Other journalists followed but not with quite the same extravagance. Members of the caseroom continued with the criticism. McNamara had until then been tolerated as a communist because he had been needed. But now he was disposable and it is always a delight of non-political persons to dispose of communists once they have served their function. Yet not one member of the workforce had the courage to state that the reason for their hostility to McNamara was his Communist Party allegiance. As for Armstrong, he was loathed because he was totally and brutally honest. He believed he would be removed not because of his toe-treading habits but because he was a Roman Catholic. I saw or heard no evidence to support his fears.

Maxwell, as I had expected, joined the attack on Armstrong. He leaned forward on the table with his white knuckles taking the weight.

"Here we have a so-called responsible councillor who will not admit to having made a mistake. We all make mistakes, but not our Mr Columbo (a reference to the TV detective). He makes no mistakes but blames the hard-working editorial for the consequences of his follies."

Then his jesting stopped. "These two men are the enemies of the co-operative. They have made a contribution in the past but they are doing you no good now. They have to be removed."

McNamara was removed on the first ballot, by a whisker. It was the first of a long series of disappointments. Nominations soon poured in to fill the vacancy and, among the first, that of Robert Maxwell. His speech acceptance was a masterpiece of modesty. It had not been his intention to seek office. In fact he had already resigned both from the council and the co-chairmanship.

"However, there seems to be evidence that most of you genuinely wish me to help you and I cannot possibly turn away from such an invitation and responsibility. After all, I am partly responsible for you being here at all. If it is your wish I shall allow my name to go forward. In all probability I shall resign at the first opportunity and allow you to conduct your co-operative (*pause*), our co-operative, in your own way, but really you must improve on your control of the company's finances. That must be your first priority. (*Another eloquent pause.*) Yes, in the interests of yourselves I accept nomination."

Most of the active trade unionists saw the speech as a model of phoney baloney. But there were the self-deluding innocents who applauded his selflessness.

Another seven nominations came in. Then came the crunch. I committed one of the worst mistakes I have ever made. According to the rules of the election the returned members of the council – that is, all the shop-floor members with the exception of McNamara – ought to have been excluded from the ballot having already secured their vote of confidence. Under pressure from the entire meeting, I allowed all the members' names to be included on the ballot paper. It is one of these moments I have regretted ever since, but as things turned out in the long run I do not believe they would have gone differently. But it is about the only time I can remember allowing myself to be stampeded by a mob out of my normal judgment. When Maxwell's nomination was made I tried to rule it out of order, but I already knew that my objections were not valid. By an unfortunate quirk of the Articles of Association, it was permissible for him to stand as an employee representative and to sit on the council as such. Dorman, quite correctly but no doubt with regret, had to over-rule me.

When Goldberg's nomination was made I reminded the members of the previous agreement that members of the executive ought not to stand for the council: they could not possibly stand for the rank and file. Now when the issue had been discussed in the Action Committee, the two strongest voices arguing for this ruling to be included in the Articles of Association had been Goldberg and Blyth. Yet here was Goldberg now actually accepting nominations, despite his loudly protested principles of the day before. There was an understanding silence when I reminded the meeting of their previous rulings, even though they had not been included in the Articles.

The silence was broken by Blyth who protested that since the ruling had not been included in the Articles, and since its exclusion had been mainly my responsibility, the nomination was in order.

"I think Mr Mackie ought to be honest here." He claimed that it was on my insistence that the management team were to be allowed to seek election to the council. I found this a shocking statement. It completely confused the membership. Russell demanded an explanation for Blyth's volte face. But all the debate did was to confuse the members further. It left them with a feeling that somehow all was not well within the council and that they were losing their grip with all their in-fighting. Blyth often called on people to be honest. The obvious implication was that they were not. Had the claim been made openly we would have challenged it unanimously.

The ballot resulted in the election of Blyth, Russell, Goldberg, Lindsay, myself and, tailing last, Maxwell. There was a momentary sweat as the votes were being counted. Maxwell was only seven votes ahead of Galt and there had to be a recount before the result was declared. I believe Armstrong was placed after Galt, but I do not remember the actual voting numbers.

Immediately after the meeting of the employees, the outside shareholders' meeting was held. I made a reasonably honest report on the state of the company without giving all the details. This was not enough for Jessica Barrett of the *Express*. As a £25 shareholder she demanded to exercise her right to know the exact circulation figures. It was my suspicion that the figures were being sought for the benefit of the Beaverbrook people; so I was not prepared to part with the information. My retreat was to promise to appraise the members of the Investors' Council, once it was elected, with all the details. My formula, thank God, was accepted. Our earlier canvassing proved a qualified success. Of the short-leet of nominees for the Investors' Council all but one were elected: Jimmy Milne, then general secretary-elect of the STUC; Billy Wolfe; Dennis Canavan, the Labour MP; and William Bargh, a co-operative organiser and former Glasgow headmaster. Only Maxwell succeeded in disrupting our slate: he was elected in preference to our other nominee, a trade union activist.

Immediately after the shareholders' meeting I made tracks for the council room. Maxwell followed at my heels. There were two or three FoCs present. Maxwell broke the ice by joking that he had noticed I had six votes cast against me, while Blyth had only four. "What does that tell us, I wonder?"

He was at his most friendly but I had no stomach for his charm.

I replied: "I had only five votes cast against me: yours doesn't count. But what I want to ask you is when do you intend to resign from the Labour Party? You are no socialist; you are at heart a fascist. If you were an honest man you would tear up your Labour Party membership card and take up membership of the National Front, for that is where your heart belongs."

By this time quite a few FoCs had gathered. They waited in

silence for Maxwell's reaction. He came quickly to the boil. He threw back his chair, leaned across it menacingly, and stabbed a warning finger at me.

"I warn you, Mackie. Two of your colleagues who opposed me have now been removed. If you continue to oppose me you will be the next to go."

I didn't feel angry, only tired and deflated. "Please leave the room. You are a disgusting person and we want to get on with our business."

He went with a bang of the door behind him as we started to discuss what tactics we could employ to remove him completely from the scene. His scraping through on a recount had given our morale a slight boost. But the election of Goldberg on the council meant he had another friend in addition to Blyth among us. There was no cause for a celebration.

A PRESS conference had been arranged to give the reporters an up-date. As usual there was a good turn-out and, again as usual, I took the chair. The members of the press had for a while enjoyed baiting Maxwell. He always played the role of an irascible bear. Alastair Balfour, then of the *Scotsman* and a personal friend, asked Maxwell about his position in the company.

"I am still a member of the executive council."

The rest of us had always called it the Works Council.

"And you are still co-chairman?"

"Of course. You may have heard rumours of my resignation. Indeed, I offered to resign but the offer was not taken up. I am still the co-chairman."

I leaned over him ingratiatingly and said: "If there is doubt in Mr Maxwell's mind, and that seems to be the case, then I will clarify the position for the benefit of him and for yourselves. Mr Maxwell offered his resignation and I accepted it. If you wish it, I accept it at this moment. There is no longer the office of co-chairman. I am the sole chairman."

It was a cheap score that gave me no satisfaction. The papers reported the events from the angle that it was a victory of the workers over Maxwell. It was no victory. But really Maxwell was not our only enemy. We had more to fear from the falling circulation and the declining revenue. Some of our councillors argued that the unwillingness of companies to advertise meant that the Establishment was out to get us. I do not believe that this was ever the case. The truth was that we did not have a fixed circulation or an identifiable readership. All groups read our paper, from bank managers to policemen to building labourers. This mixing of social groups gave little advantage to the advertiser. If he wanted to sell a quality house, he would choose the *Herald* or the *Scotsman*. If he wanted to recruit labourers he would go to the *Record*. Though we covered all the groups our figure for each did not justify placing an advertisement. Maxwell kept promising he could raise advertising. Time proved that he could not but our workforce were not to discover this until it was too late.

CHAPTER SIXTEEN

He's quite mad, you know

THE FOLLOWING morning I discussed the sad day's events with Eric Tough. By this time he was more than ever opposed to Maxwell. He smiled ruefully as I walked into his office. "A bad day's work," he said. The first thing to do, I replied, was to let the Government know of the latest turn of the events. That morning I sent Tony Benn a personal letter, marked strictly private and confidential. I could not even let the other members of the council see it, because Maxwell would have blocked it. Therefore I sent it as a personal statement.

In the letter I told Benn that by dint of disrupting the annual general meeting Maxwell had succeeded in having himself voted on to the council as a worker-director. In effect this meant that the shop-floor representation on the ten-man council had been reduced to five. This was "a very dangerous position in respect of their having a built-in permanent majority for the shop-floor." (With Maxwell's election the council's composition had become five workers, two members of the Investors' Council, the editor and the general manager and, of course, Maxwell. Thus the shop-floor had lost already its built-in majority.)

We had learned, I wrote, that Maxwell had been doing the rounds in London, telling everybody that the paper was almost finished, that it was in a total state of collapse. In addition, statements had been made to the press, some of which we had been able to trace back to Maxwell, that our trading position was far worse than we admitted. This was very damaging and bad for morale. I was particularly concerned about the latest allegation that while he wanted to take immediate action to increase revenue we were content to wait until September. This was manifestly untrue and I listed the steps we had already taken – our advertising presentations, the launch of competitions, radio advertising, the employment of more sales representatives. We had also hired a firm of professional market researchers to do a readership survey. Based on its results we would take steps to improve editorial content. The only thing we would postpone until September would be any major changes to the paper, such as going tabloid.

Maxwell, I continued, had made or was making proposals that would seriously affect the viability of the company. I listed them: a 24-hour paper, which would rapidly bleed our cash resources; postponement of the launch, which would have cost the company £120,000; a cut in the selling price from 6p to 5p, which would have cut circulation revenue by 16½%, and an unspecified reduction in advertising rates; and more staff in certain departments. Furthermore he had committed the company without reference to the Works Council to organising trade missions to Russia, the Middle East and America at "God only knows what cost".

The letter went on: "I have no wish at this stage to create undue alarm; yet were I not to sound the alarm bells, I would not be fulfilling the responsibilities that were placed on me . . . My personal position is that I shall remain to fight him and his influence on the council." Finally I told him that if Maxwell were to control the company it was inevitable we should lose the bulk of our management team. "Sorry to sound so pessimistic but we will take the rascal on and beat him. If you want a confidential meeting we will be delighted to arrange one at any time."

WE HADN'T long to wait for Maxwell's next move. Only a week later a 1200-word telex arrived. It said he had received only that morning the agenda for the Works Council meeting to be held that day in Glasgow at 2.30pm. Because of the short notice he had not been able to re-arrange his schedule. He therefore asked us to accept the meeting was not properly convened and was not empowered to transact formal business. A further serious irregularity was that the council had never been given an opportunity formally to approve the minutes of the previous meeting. He therefore asked for all previous minutes to be circulated so that they could be approved or amended at the next properly convened meeting.

After giving his version of events at the AGM, he said that I had shown stubborn determination to prevent his playing a positive part in saving the *News*. He hoped I would accept the decision of the workforce and do what was necessary to establish a harmonious working relationship. He then detailed a plan of action which included the following points:

1. The executive council was the supreme policy-making body. The co-chairmen and the general manager would implement its decisions.

2. As one of the co-chairmen he would be responsible for the commercial policies of the paper. I would be responsible for relations with the workforce, trade unions and shareholders.

3. The general manager would have day-to-day operating control. The editor would be in sole control of contents.

4. He was confident that within the next four-to-six weeks he could increase the volume of advertising by at least 50% and by 75% within ten weeks.

5. The paper would be relaunched by the end of October with a relaunch expenditure of £200,000.

6. Its price would be reduced to 5p under the slogan, "The SDN helps to fight inflation by reducing its price to 5p."

7. He was prepared to devote the bulk of his time for the next three months to the affairs of the *News*. He hoped this would mend the rift between us and save the paper from extinction by slow death.

8. Mr Dallas and Mr Tough should be able to confirm that our losses were running at between £15/20,000 a week. This was "one hell of a sum" and far worse than the report issued by Mr Tough to the workforce.

My first reaction was of raised hackles then bemused incredulity. Russell said Maxwell had gone off his head. "He's quite mad you know." At the meeting Goldberg quipped: "I see Big Bob is at it again. When will he learn that we are not here only at his bidding?"

Russell challenged him at once. Some members of the workforce, he said, had been leaked copies and it had caused panic in some quarters. Was Goldberg prepared to stand up to Maxwell? There was no clear answer.

It was the usual run-of-the-mill sort of meeting. I reported that Bruce Millan, then Minister of State at the Scottish Office, had promised we would be put on the schedule for Government advertising. Up to that point we hadn't qualified because we couldn't prove our circulation figures: we needed six months' performance as evidence of them. Tough reported that System Three Scotland had been commissioned to conduct the readership survey.

Officially unknown to myself, although I was well aware of their activities, a small group of the workforce attempted to take the issue of Maxwell's election into their own hands. By this time Armstrong had left his job. His defeat in the election had hurt more than he was prepared to admit. McNamara and he, together with some others, held an unofficial meeting of the workforce in the reel-room. It was not well attended but attracted most of the activists among the workforce. They discussed the possibility of bringing the workforce out on strike to remove Maxwell. The result was inconclusive. Apart from this meeting I am unaware of any other activity organised by them.

JIMMY ROY had been working under an enormous amount of pressure as production manager without a deputy. The names of two contenders had been discussed by the council, which agreed to advertise the vacancy in the press and ask the two to apply for it also.

After the meeting Russell approached me and said: "You know Charlie Armstrong has left his job on account of Maxwell?" It was more of a rebuke than a question. Of course, I replied. No-one, not even Jimmy Roy, knew more about the mechanics of the building. Russell reminded me of my responsibilities. I must forget the other candidate to whom I'd already spoken. The office of chairman transcended personal feelings. I knew no-one could touch Charlie on his knowledge and ability.

He was right and I agreed that we needed Charlie more than ever before but worried that were we to appoint him it could be construed as a backdoor method of re-instating him. But we were not in the business of appeasing people, we were in the business of survival. Some hard decisions would have to be taken. Armstrong was capable of tackling the editorial, no doubt about that. The journalists still reserved a special hell for him because of his outspoken-ness and his criticisms of them for not having the spirit of a co-operative. Another area of ill-feeling against him was the caseroom. He had constantly accused them of wanting only a job and wishing to continue their employment as if they still worked for Beaverbrook. In the Action Committee days he had unearthed a letter sent by Ray Chard to the caseroom proposing the establishment of a power block between the two departments, once the paper was under way. Armstrong had never forgotten the occasion and had constantly warned everyone against the danger. His problem was that he was too honest at times. Such people are born to be crucified.

In the meantime, along with Ian Bain, the financial controller, I prepared a report on Maxwell's proposal to reduce the price of the paper to 5p. Bain's figures staggered me. Given a circulation of 150,000, another 67,000 copies would have to be sold merely to recoup the lost revenue and we would still be in the same sad mess.

THE REPORT by System Three began to filter in. There were no objections to the price of the paper. But too many readers were buying the paper out of a sense of sympathy with our fight or because they believed in the co-operative structure. For most it was a second paper. There were also serious criticisms of the content. Our readers did not want the paper to be blatantly either Left or Right. They wanted us to report news as it happened, without bias or comment. There were favourable comments about the sports coverage and our blue thistle logo was popular.

Tough, having right-wing views anyway, repeatedly complained about the leftward lurches the paper took from time to time, depending on who happened to be in charge on the editorial floor. At the time I agreed with this concern. Sometimes the journalists gave a left-wing slant to their stories, which did nothing to add to the credibility of the paper among readers or advertisers. And it was a betrayal of our early boast that we would produce a paper that was free of political cant. I was in a peculiar attitude politically. My own sympathies lay with those of some of the journalists but they were helping nobody. I believe that all the Left argument needs is coverage. The weight of its logic is its propaganda value. Had the journalists simply been capable of presenting an objective report then the interests of the Left would have been well served. It is only right-wing policies that require dressing up. They normally die under exposure. Over a few weeks the paper had campaigned for improvements to the A74 south, which seemed to be plagued by accidents. The Scottish Office published in response a report on its accident rating. This showed that taking into account its traffic density it was one of the safest roads in Scotland. Goldberg, when he told me of the findings, said they would not publish them but continue with the campaign. "It wouldn't help the paper if the report was published," he said. That would be dishonest, I said. He shrugged his shoulders, grinned, and made no further comment.

In his company report Tough referred to the System Three findings and appealed to the journalists not to let their personal political outlook spill into the news columns. But with the lack of editorial discipline, the message passed unheeded.

CHAPTER SEVENTEEN

A topsy-turvy world

June 18

THE CIRCULATION had fallen to around 135,000. It was a far cry from the days of hope and shallow boasts. In every department men were again justifiably worried about unemployment. And their fears were fast becoming father of unreason. There was obviously a basic fault, but they wondered what it was. They had already made sacrifices of Armstrong and McNamara: what else could be sacrificed now? They could not within themselves accept the System Three findings that 70% of our readers were not happy with the standard of journalism. There was no simple solution to that complaint. Already it was evident that more money would be needed before long to carry the paper until it found its feet. That morning a meeting of the Works Council was held. Jimmy Milne and Willie Bargh were attending for the first time as representatives of the Investors' Council. Maxwell unexpectedly turned up.

From the outset the newcomers, used to orderly meetings, were stunned by his conduct and his blatant bad manners as he challenged my every ruling. He demanded that the last meeting be written off as *ultra vires*. I wasn't quite sure what that meant and I stalled to confirm that he believed it to have been unconstitutional. His claim was based on the short notice given of the meeting. We checked: it had been 72 hours – enough even for him. His objections were swept aside. We moved to the first item on the agenda, the appointment of a chairman. I recalled that Mr Maxwell had already resigned as co-chairman and I was the sole chairman; the office of co-chairman no longer existed.

Maxwell blustered his protest. His co-chairmanship was in the prospectus. There was no alternative. But Russell moved that the office of co-chairman be eliminated. Agreed. Bargh took over the chair from me and asked for nominations. First I was nominated by Russell supported by Lindsay; then to my surprise Blyth allowed himself to be nominated by Goldberg seconded by Maxwell. Including his own vote, Blyth received only three votes while I received the support of all the others.

Maxwell again took up the injustice of not being allowed to continue in office as co-chairman. Eventually Bargh cut him short. "You have done nothing," he said, "to convince me that you are a fit person to hold the office of chairman, particularly considering that this company is a co-operative."

Maxwell changed his tack. Now that he was a workers' member of the council, "with the overwhelming support of the workforce", he wished to take his place on the Works Council. He therefore resigned forthwith from the Investors' Council.

Russell and I pointed out that he been elected only after a recount. Still he was not silenced. Why had his telex not been discussed at the last meeting of the Works Council? That was far more important for it had proposed a relaunch on the slogan that the *News* was for securing employment. Yet we had not even discussed it.

Sillitto stirred himself wearily. Before we could relaunch we had to have a new product to offer. "It is not enough simply to ride a white charger about the evils of unemployment. Every newspaper in the country is concerned about the problem."

Maxwell pounced. "The *News,* Fred, if you had allowed me to finish, will also lead a campaign against inflation. We will set the ball rolling with the slogan, The *Daily News* fights inflation, by reducing the price of the paper."

Russell pointed out the extent of the revenue loss and declared that you could not reconcile a campaign against unemployment and reduce the price of the paper at the same time. "Your proposals will create unemployment – it will close the paper down and we'll all be unemployed." The discussion was getting nowhere. I tried to set the proposal aside for the moment. But Maxwell kept the pot stirring. He said he would put before us proposals that would allow him personally to publish an evening paper. With the council's consent he would hire the plant and labour from the co-operative at a reasonable price. "Now what more can I do for you than that?"

By this time we had had enough of his bantering and filibustering. Setting aside my usual role of mediator and diplomat, I caustically informed him that I would believe his good intentions when I had a chance to examine his proposals. Until then we would carry on with running a morning paper.

Maxwell complained about everyone mistrusting him but promised to have substantial proposals before long. They were never made. In fits and starts we got through the rest of the business but not until Maxwell had insisted that regular mass meetings of the workforce be held to keep them informed of the state of the company. I agreed with the proposal and turned immediately to Jimmy Crossan and landed him with the responsibility, as imperial father, of convening the meetings. He looked perplexed but, sensing I had an ulterior motive, immediately agreed.

Afterwards he approached me. "I take it you don't want to convene the meetings yourself on account of Maxwell?" he asked. I tried to explain my fears. We had, I said, never enjoyed the full support of the workforce for our concept of a co-operative. Almost half of them would rather have traditional management, which they could confront, rather than be involved in management themselves. None of us could blame them. Society, the trade union movement, our educational system, the mass media, indeed everything in life, told us that the correct form of management was one of employer and employee. Some of our bitterest opponents when we were trying to raise cash had been active communists. We had no right, they said, to create an island of socialism in the sea of capitalism. Jimmy and I had never listened but the others had to: their belief was in employment, not in co-operatives. The tragedy was that they did not seem to realise that our only hope of continuing in employment lay within the structure of a co-operative, which given time and prosperity would be secure.

"But in times of economic hardship our workforce believe they have an alternative they can turn to – Maxwell and traditional management. We know that Maxwell would ruin the paper they don't. We have told them what he is like but they choose not to believe us."

In one of his books Dostoevsky states that the bounds of a man's credulity are contained within the bounds of his personal experience. Our members didn't realise what Maxwell was like because they had

174

never met anyone like him. They were therefore susceptible to trusting him. We offered an untried formula, the co-operative; he offered traditional employment. "We can't blame the workforce if they prefer Maxwell's offer," I concluded. "He knows this all too clearly. He sees the weaknesses in our set-up and intends to exploit them with fears of insecurity and unemployment. That is why he wants the mass meetings, to feed the members with fear of the council and eventually hostility to it."

For all my working life I had advocated mass meetings of the workforce, yet here I was opposing them. We had stumbled into a topsy-turvy world.

Times were very trying, very disheartening. The fall in sales, and advertising, continued. Despite pressure the Government advertising agencies still did not deliver many advertisements. In this respect we were let down badly. The Government had shown a certain courage and conviction when they had given us the loan but they had not the staying power to see the thing through. Had they given us the same advertising the other Scottish dailies were receiving at the time it might have encouraged other advertisers to take space.

To compound the problem, the promotion of Armstrong, as I had feared, was causing a lot of friction. Russell had proposed Armstrong at a council meeting. Few could argue that he was not the man for the job but there had been opposition from some of the councillors. Maxwell, Blyth and Goldberg argued that to consider him was an affront to the workforce since they had already rejected him. There was also the argument that Russell was pushing for Armstrong because he would be a weapon with which we could fight against Maxwell. It was true: he would have been of enormous strength against Maxwell and his acolytes. When the vote was put there was a tie. I had already decided to give my vote to Armstrong, accepting that there would be a near-riot. We had to make the correct choice and set aside the consequences. I cast my vote in favour of him and it was agreed to make the first approach to him. The decision proved to be yet another whip with which to lash the council. Eventually there was so much uproar, even among the FoCs, that its implementation had to be postponed.

The meeting with the FoCs on this issue revealed a fundamental problem to me. In a vote they decided there was no need for an assistant production manager: they were against Armstrong's appointment but hadn't the courage to say so. After the vote I thanked Crossan, who had chaired the meeting, and thanked them for their advice which would be conveyed to the council. But, I said, the council might still go ahead with the appointment.

McAskill, his face tensed with anger, demanded: "Is Mr Mackie telling this meeting that he will not necessarily abide by its decision?"

You can't avoid every explosion. "That's right," I said.

"In that case I'll be reporting back to my chapel to see what they say about it. They are not going to accept this lying down."

I looked at him. "Doddy, you must do what you must do and I what I must do. I will not interfere with the running of your chapel. In return I ask you not to interfere in the functions of the council."

Up to this point I had tried to contain Maxwell's influence. I had failed: it had grown. Now I decided to go on to the attack. I set up a meeting with the caseroom, still an area of his strongest support. Here Eric Tough and I laid it on the line. We told them what Maxwell's game was, what his proposals had been and the effect they would have had. There were no indications of hostility to us from any of the compositors yet I knew he had plenty of support there. They listened to what we had to say; some asked questions that indicated their personal mistrust of Maxwell. But the passive majority listened and said nothing. It is difficult to fight an enemy who doesn't come out into the open and identify himself. The caseroom attitude was totally at odds with their trade union. Fred Smith, then general secretary of the Scottish Graphical Association, gave specific instructions to his members that they were to give me their total support. His instructions were ignored to the point that they were not even discussed. A meeting with the clerical chapel was quite different. Here the opposition to Maxwell was almost total. It was music to hear the young girls sound off against the man they had identified as the common enemy – Robert Maxwell. Yet we all realised that he was gaining ground among the workforce. It was being done in stealth, by his supporters, by discrediting the council and undermining trust in it.

JUST AS it was becoming increasingly difficult to live, so it was becoming all the more necessary to make plans for the future. The final

System Three report was made available. As we had expected, about 75% of our readers either would prefer or would be just as happy with a tabloid newspaper. The reasons were obvious. Tabloids are easier to read on public transport and in factory toilets (where, it seemed, most of the national popular dailies were digested). They carried briefer stories and therefore more of them. It wasn't what most of us on the Works Council would have preferred but that had nothing to do with the outcome. We were in the business of survival. But Tough, Russell and I, agreeing with the notion of a tabloid relaunch, argued more strongly than ever that the main problem remained the quality of the editorial content. We could change the wrapping but if the same puerile commodity was inside it then there could be no hope.

Tough, without waiting for an official decision by the council, and with my personal support, set up two working parties. One was to look at the editorial side, with Goldberg in charge. The other, under Jimmy Roy, considered the technical problems. At this stage we didn't know if a tabloid could be produced by our existing machinery. The verdict from the machine room and the caseroom was positive. Our attitude at the beginning of the struggle had always been one of firstly deciding a target date. Working out how to achieve it came later. The principle had never let us down. The workforce were capable of fantastic efforts and results. Indeed they preferred to tackle the impossible. The job satisfaction in itself was the reward. I told a meeting of FoCs that the London *Evening News* had taken about 18 months to convert from broadsheet to tabloid. They agreed to have the conversion completed in three weeks. And they did! No other workforce in the world under any system known have matched their performance. Tough said: "It's up to the editorial now."

AT LAST we were able to propose to the full meeting of the council a launch date of August 18. By then holidays would be largely over. We hoped the public would be in the mood for a fresh start. Another compelling reason was that we were losing so much money that we were afraid that the Government might step in and close the paper while we still had some cash in the bank. Finally, we had to give the workforce new hope.

There was unanimous support for the proposals. It was a great chance to begin again. Goldberg was taking more and more editorial responsibility. Some of us were doubtful of his ability to make mature judgments but we were relieved he was prepared to make judgments of any sort. Too much had been shelved. The System Three report had not made good reading. More than 70% of our regular readers thought the paper less than good. Most bought it because of the history of the struggle that had given it birth, or because of the co-operative structure, or simply because it was Scottish. This was no base on which to build a viable company.

By this time Tough and I had got into the habit of discussing our private worlds. They could hardly have been further apart. His salary was about £10,000: I was paid £60 a week. And that was only the beginning of our differences. Yet we evolved a very close relationship. One day he told me that Ralph Saunders, a former *Express* journalist had written from Cornwall asking for a job. He showed me the letter. Saunders had been a good sub in the old *Express* days. He had just returned from Australia, where he had been editor of a tabloid and doubled its circulation. He had now closeted himself in an attic somewhere in Cornwall to write a book. He seemed just the man for us, and I said so.

Tough noticed that this was his second letter and that, according to it, he had received no reply to his first, which had been addressed to Denny Macgee. "Let's hope it just got lost," said Tough.

Sillitto was consulted and agreed that Saunders should be consulted with a view to offering him an executive post. Wishing to avoid another Mary Holland situation, Tough and I swore him to secrecy and met him in the bar at Glasgow Airport. As luck would have it, we found ourselves in the middle of a mob of photographers waiting for a Japanese ballet dancer. Among the pressmen were two from the *News*. I told them a fib about waiting for a relative. Just then Saunders arrived but luckily no-one recognised him. He was a man of about 40, crew cut, his old leanness beginning to show signs of a paunch. We told him what had happened to Mary Holland, of the problems of editorial executive control, of Maxwell's involvement.

He gave an amused smile. "Look, lads, I know these men. I worked with them for years, didn't I?"

Tough warned him: "You'll find an almost animal-like hostility from the existing editorial executives. It won't be personal. It's a form of defence mechanism."

"I've handled all sorts of queer bastards in my day," Saunders replied.

Within a week he took up his responsibilities. He loved the idea of the challenge. But he just as quickly sickened. Within days every area of his authority was being challenged by his fellow executives, mainly Goldberg. The editor and the council had agreed to pay him the same rate as the top executives. The chapel protested and Sillitto gave into their demands, cutting the rate. Before the council could rally to his support, Saunders packed his bags and returned to Cornwall. Most of this I learned from second hand when I returned from a holiday. Russell called the incident a conspiracy of incompetence. When I heard of it I felt as sick as ever I had done. The editorial executives would never allow an injection of fresh talent and without it we were in deep trouble.

CHAPTER EIGHTEEN

A rogue elephant

July 29

A MASS meeting had been called for the following day so that the workforce could be informed of and involved with the switch to tabloid. Maxwell used the meeting to make another grab for control. On the evening of the 29th he turned up without informing any but a few. Blyth happened to be working late that night and was there to greet him on his arrival.

The place was jumping with excitement as Maxwell went from one department to another asking for on-the-spot chapel meetings. He introduced himself to everyone within reach like an American presidential candidate. He told a caseroom meeting that the only hope for survival was for him to be given complete control and for Mackie and his friends to be removed. In return he guaranteed all the advertising we could possibly handle and an immediate cash investment of £500,000. All but a few swallowed his spiel – hook, line and sinker.

The councillors met in the morning. Maxwell tried to dominate the proceedings. He said the tabloid relaunch was a waste of time and moved that the starting date be put back to September: there wasn't enough time. But, Tough explained with fraying patience, it was too late for any further delay. The workforce were impatient and an advertising campaign was already going ahead.

With the meeting nearly finished Maxwell asked to be excused to attend a Natsopa committee meeting. I decided to accompany him to make sure he stuck to the facts. There were around a dozen members present, with McAskill in the chair. He opened the meeting with an openly hostile glance at Maxwell who, with an ingratiating smile that did not reach his eyes, repeated the proposals he had put to the caseroom the night before.

I intervened. I did not believe he could bring in advertisements. "You haven't brought in one yet. And you couldn't raise a penny of additional investment. Tell our friends just where the money is coming from and put their minds at ease."

Maxwell complained about my intrusion but McAskill demanded that he answer.

"Don't worry, I can raise the cash all right. How much cash can Mackie raise for you?"

"Two and a half million up till now," replied McAskill. "You must tell us where all this extra money is supposed to be coming from and that you claim you can raise."

McAskill had him on a spit and wouldn't let him go. Eventually Maxwell, with a resigned shake of his head, said: "All right, since you press me, there are three sources – Beaverbrook, the Government, and I can raise another few thousand on the market."

He said it with a pronounced lack of conviction. It was a bad meeting for him and he knew it. Perhaps if I could get the same message across to the workforce I could still forestall his bid for power.

We made our way up to the editorial floor where the mass meeting was to be held. Waiting for the lift Maxwell and I found ourselves together and alone.

"I take it," I asked, "that you are going to use the meeting to make a bid for the control of the company?"

He smiled, I believe genuinely, nodded his head and admitted: "That's right."

In my pocket I carried my "speech", in fact an aide memoire of subject headings. I tried to concentrate on the problems facing the company and made no reference to Maxwell. I hoped the members would see that he was irrelevant. I got a good hearing. The workforce started to throw in some good ideas about what might be done to facilitate the change-over. The meeting was going badly for Maxwell as it became more evident, as it went on, that he was superfluous to our problems.

So he rose to speak. I knew, we all knew, that it was going to be dirty from here in. It might be, he said, that the future of the paper would depend on the tabloid relaunch.

"But let us not forget who the people responsible for the crisis are. They are here at the top table, the executive councillors who support Mackie and his mishandling of the affairs of your, of our co-operative. Mackie's answer to the crisis is to keep my employees' shares from me and to prevent me from making any contribution to the decisions of the company. I am constantly kept out in the cold. He will not even allow me to bring in advertising, and you all know that the loss of advertising revenue is one of the basic causes of the crisis."

His harangue continued for perhaps another 10 minutes. It was badly constructed, full of contradictions and repetitions. But it served to rouse the blood of his supporters. He made no mention of the promised £500,000. He was very careful about that, allowing his disciples to carry the good news by word of mouth. I was accused of seeking to make political capital for myself out of the paper. We were all abused. Many among the membership, particularly the FoCs, booed him as he spoke. They knew the game he was playing but their members just didn't seem to care.

Blyth backed Maxwell. He said that I (Mackie) had sworn to do everything in my power to remove Maxwell. He was sick and tired of all the wrangling in the council. We all should "be honest" with ourselves. We were in a sorry mess and the fault was the council's. We just didn't have the experience to make the right decisions. "I'm sorry to admit it, but it's true." We needed Robert Maxwell, who had proved himself a friend of the co-operative, we needed his experience. "Otherwise we are lost and our jobs are lost also."

Blyth's speech came from a member of the council who had been very active in the Action Committee. It had the effect of destroying any remaining confidence the workforce had in the co-operative structure.

Others followed in support – Macgee, Welsh. Kenny Grant, by this time head reader, made a pathetic contribution. "You must realise, Mr Chairman, that we need to feel the sting of the master's whip, we want to feel it." The tragedy was that he really believed it.

A motion from Macgee that Maxwell be restored to full executive authority in the company to assist in the re-launch was put to a vote. It was carried, but not by a convincing majority.

TWO DAYS LATER a meeting of the Works Council was held. Maxwell was after my blood. He recalled Blyth's comment that I had intended to remove him (Maxwell). He demanded to know if this was the case and that I make my position clear, particularly in view of the "overwhelming vote of confidence I received at the meeting." He turned to the stenographer and said: "I want this part of the meeting carefully minuted."

I suppose he hoped I would resign but I would not be cornered. Blyth, I said, had been inaccurate. It was no secret I was unhappy about Maxwell's presence on the council. Everyone in the workforce knew that. But I accepted the wishes of the members. "I am prepared to work alongside you for the success of the paper. That must be the over-riding consideration. Now will you work alongside me?"

But still he came back, demanding that I move a vote of confidence in him. Bargh, tired of the game, asked him to shut up and accept my statement, which was acceptable to the other members of the council.

Maxwell listened intently to the discussion on how much authority he was to have. Then he said: "The idea is that I shall come to live here in Glasgow for some months, during which time I shall do all in my power to save the paper. To do this effectively I shall have to be given executive powers. There can be no argument there. Mackie will look after the morale of the workforce. He is good at that sort of thing." I ground my teeth at his ingratiations.

Tough, he continued, would look after day-to-day management. "I shall be vested with powers to raise more cash and sell advertising space. If at any time you feel dissatisfied with my performance then it will be the easiest thing in the world to remove me. Now what more can I offer than that?"

I asked him where he would raise the cash. With a sly smile he assured us he could raise it with little difficulty. Now, he said, he would leave the room and allow us to deliberate in his absence. He had no wish to control the company and made it clear that any arrangement would be subject to his instant dismissal should he fail us in any way.

And out he went. His offer was reasonable, no doubt about that. But the problem was that few of us could trust him. As the debate progressed I became worried about the time. Tough and I had arranged to meet Bruce Millan, by this time Secretary of State for Scotland, at St Andrew's House in Edinburgh. We wanted to sound out the Government about an overdraft to help us with cash-flow, assuming the re-launch proved a success. Only Russell among the other councillors knew of the meeting. We didn't want Maxwell to hear of it because he would insist on coming along. I asked for an adjournment so that we could leave. Blyth and Goldberg demanded to know where we were going and why. I wouldn't concede the information, and their shouting became louder and louder. I was accused by Goldberg of megalomania, of seeking only self-aggrandisement. Knowing that I had the majority anyway, I put the matter to a vote and won it despite their loud protests.

When we arrived at St Andrew's House we discovered that Maxwell, though absent from the room at the time, had been quick to guess at the reasons for our absence. Millan with whom I had enjoyed an acquaintanceship since we had been in the Labour League of Youth some 25 years previously, told us that he had already been on the phone asking for a meeting but the request had been turned down. It was one of those not rare moments when I admired Maxwell's skill. I believe he had deduced our intentions and had taken steps to beat us to the Minister. I appreciate that sort of cunning.

In the event the meeting proved fruitless. Millan told us that as things stood there was no hope of further Government aid. If the paper was starved for cash but at the same time doing well the Government might find it hard to turn us down.

When we reported back to the council, our explanations for leaving were accepted and, surprisingly, understood. I believe Maxwell had discussed the probability of our arrangement and had pointed out to Blyth and Goldberg that our actions had been correct.

The debate about Maxwell's powers resumed. He now took part in it himself. He would ensure that the tabloid would go out on time, ensure that it was editionised properly, improve classified advertising. He would engage extra staff and personally contact top advertisers.

Blyth said the offer could not possibly be turned down. Russell stated there should be a full meeting of shareholders since the proposal represented so fundamental a change in the company's structure. But to me the debate was so basic. If executive authority was to be given to Maxwell then it would be the end of our concept of a co-operative.

Then Tough made his position clear. If Maxwell were engaged on the terms proposed he would consider himself superfluous to the needs of the company.

Maxwell again tried to clarify his position. "Really, I shall be able to stay on only some four or six weeks. We shall need a manager. Let's not be hasty."

Russell by now had to leave to do his evening stint at his desk. He left me his mandated vote. Now it was my turn to state my views. I argued that I had learned never to trust Maxwell. If any authority at all was given to him it would mean the end of the co-operative since he would not stop until he had complete and absolute control. The choice was therefore one of complete control to Maxwell or none at all. You cannot satisfy the insatiable.

On a motion put by Blyth that Maxwell should be given executive powers to be decided at a later meeting, the voting was 5-2 in favour, Russell's vote and mine being cast against. Now the trouble would start. Maxwell had the strength and vitality of a rogue elephant. But no-one ever successfully saddled a rogue elephant.

For some time my health had been deteriorating. Normally I enjoy reasonable health but my life had not been normal for a long time. My problem is that I have only one kidney, the other having been lost because of tuberculosis years ago. In fact both my kidneys had been rotted by the disease on two occasions, but my left had survived and although crippled has kept me going along happily for many years. But if I am subjected to great pressure it decides to misbehave. No doubt there is a perfectly logical medical reason and it never worries me. I get over the problem by simply having a rest. But this time it had been troubling me for too long. I needed a break. My brother-in-law had offered me for a few days the use of his caravan at Inverbervie in the north-east of Scotland. I accepted the invitation. The council had decided to invest Maxwell with certain restricted powers. Let them get on with it. I don't seek to defend my decision. It was born of a fatigue and irresistible tiredness that demanded that I rest and regenerate my battered spirits. So off I went over the weekend.

But it was no real holiday. Daily I phoned in for the latest news. Russell told me of the council meeting held on August 6. It had almost turned out to be abortive. Bargh had threatened resignation if Maxwell were given overwhelming power. Maxwell demanded yet another mass meeting to let the workforce determine his powers. My absence, he said, clearly indicated that I was unwilling to work alongside him.

What I had said at the last meeting was proving to be correct. Either Maxwell would be given complete authority or none. Tough now resigned because he considered the vote of the workforce to be a vote of no confidence in himself. As far as he was concerned Maxwell was the new general manager.

Explaining his reasons to the press, Tough made rather an odd statement. He did mention Maxwell's involvement, it is true, but he went on to complain about the Works Council's interference with management functions, even to the point of having a debate on the price of pies in the canteen. Certainly it is true that initially we had to organise the launch of the paper. That was not by design, it came out of necessity. But I can recall no other occasion when we did not support him in his management decisions. The point about the price of pies was correct. But the debate went much wider. It was about whether or not the company should subsidise the canteen, and the decision could not possibly be left to Tough's sole discretion.

Maxwell latched on to Tough's resignation and demanded another mass meeting unless he were given the authority that Tough had previously wielded. This demand brought protests from Bargh that no company could be run on the basis of mass meetings.

ON REFLECTION I'm glad I missed it. I read in the other dailies the statement on Maxwell's responsibilities issued to the press. It said that the council had decided to invite Maxwell to resume executive powers "as they may be assigned to him" by the council, to assist in the tabloid launch. The council had asked him to assist the paper to build up its circulation and increase its advertising revenue. He had agreed to undertake the task and would be devoting the bulk of his time in Glasgow to it over the next two or three months.

It read strangely when I first saw it. In fact nothing had been decided since I had left. The council had still to make up its mind and it couldn't. It was caught in a dilemma of its own making. Relaxing in the sun, playing with my son of only a few months, I wondered just what the next step would be. Maxwell must have been happy with the press release or it wouldn't have gone out. Would he now seize power? Russell, when I phoned him, said he suspected this would be the case. Prodded by my conscience I then took the decision to pack up and return before the week was out.

Russell sounded distraught.

"Are you sure you still intend to fight him, Allister?"

"Of course I shall. You should know by this time that I won't accept him in any circumstances."

There was a long pause.

"Well, all right then. But it is going to be very difficult for you. If you don't go along with him he'll try to destroy you. And he'll almost certainly succeed. He now has the support of the membership."

I didn't feel upset at Russell's fears for me or of his failure to understand and know me. We are all strangers to everyone, particularly to ourselves. Under pressure of the sort that Maxwell had mounted they could not anticipate my reactions. Only I knew myself, and then only in an imprecise, unproven way. Some time later I was approached by a stranger who asked me if I knew Allister Mackie. "Yes I do," I replied. "But, believe me, only vaguely."

CHAPTER NINETEEN

A blind faith

EVEN AS Russell and I were speaking on the phone Maxwell was assuming an authority no-one had dreamed of giving him. He met representatives of the newsagents' federation. He asked for their full support in the relaunch and promised them special terms if they helped in the campaign. They agreed. They were pleased to have been given their place in the scheme of things. But their goodwill was short-lived for within an hour Maxwell had gone to a semi-public meeting with advertising agents and announced that he intended to reduce the price of the paper to 5p. And he hadn't even told the Works Council! This meant the newsagents were now committed to taking part in a campaign which would reduce their income, since their commission is linked to the price. Their support went by the board. They did not positively work against the relaunch but did not participate in the way it had been hoped. By contrast they pulled out all the stops for the *Record* a week later when it increased its selling price to 6p.

I suspect the decision to reduce the price of the paper was taken either between the two meetings or, more probably, during the course of the second meeting. From time to time we witnessed this weakness in Maxwell – a tendency to make basic decisions from the top of his head, without full and due thought about the commercial consequences. The first I heard of the intention to cut the price of the paper was when I read it in the *News* next day. I was stunned, for from that moment on there was no hope. Russell told me that Maxwell had simply breezed into a council meeting and told them of the *fait accompli*. The members had shrugged their shoulders and turned to other things.

At the same meeting Maxwell announced he had held up a

cheque for £59,000 due to Beaverbrook. When we bought the building, Beaverbrook had paid the VAT. As a matter of course we had reclaimed the money from the Government and now were due to pay it back. It was never ours but because of a slip-up by the Beaverbrook lawyers it had been omitted from the arrangements: but they nonetheless insisted that we were obliged to repay it. Maxwell's reason for holding on to it was a claim that Jocelyn Stevens had made a private deal with him. Maxwell claimed Stevens had promised that once the money had been raised from the prospectus another £40,000 would be forthcoming from Beaverbrook: he was now demanding that payment. Stevens vigorously denied ever having made the promise. I had been an accidental witness of the conversation when the two men had discussed the matter. Maxwell had been stretched out on his bed in the Albany Hotel, talking on the phone to Stevens while the adjoining room was bursting with the noise of revelry – it was just after all the money had been raised on the day the prospectus was closed.

I heard Maxwell say: "That's right, Jocelyn, we've raised the cash. What have you got to say about that, eh? You never thought we could do it? Now how about £40,000 from yourself? We're doing you a favour taking the building off your hands."

Of course I couldn't hear Stevens's replies but I was left with the impression that they were unenthusiastic. At a later stage, on the afternoon we purchased the building from Beaverbrook, Stevens asked me if Maxwell had stated that the £40,000 was due. No, he hadn't made any such claim, I replied. Stevens seemed relieved and mumbled a comment that perhaps Maxwell had been drinking at the time. But he hadn't: he had been perfectly sober.

Russell, cautious as ever, now advised the council to think carefully before they endorsed Maxwell's decision to withhold the cash but Maxwell simply told the councillors that he had already informed Stevens of his decision. At this time I knew nothing of the affair. But Russell did tell me over the phone that a huge row was brewing that could kill us off with our creditors if Maxwell got his way. He concluded: "I honestly believe he has gone off his head. It's very worrying."

I could stay on holiday no longer and returned to Albion Street. The break had done me good and I had a clearer perspective. To save the paper, if that were still possible, we had as a first priority to restore the price to 6p, improve editorial content by weeding out the editorial executive and replacing them either with existing editorial staff or by recruiting new staff, but as a necessary first step to rid the company of Maxwell.

Within two days I had returned to my desk. Maxwell looked shocking. He usually presented himself as a man with a reasonable waistline and jet black hair. This was not the man I now saw. His stomach ballooned in front of him and his sleek black hair was turning grey. Until that moment in my innocence it had never occurred to me that men could wear corsets or dye their hair.

There was no doubt that he was in complete command. Ian Bain had resigned from his dual roles of secretary and financial controller on account of Maxwell's decision to reduce the price of the paper. Maxwell had assumed the title of company secretary as well as that of chief executive. There had been no council meetings to invest him with these titles. His take-over had taken place virtually without protest or challenge from the councillors. It was total and complete, even to the extent of having given instructions to the switchboard that all incoming calls for the chairman must be directed through his own secretary. Even the plate on his office door described him as "Chief Executive".

A council meeting had been arranged for the Wednesday. I decided to use it to confront Maxwell. There was a problem. Bargh, who had become more and more antagonistic to Maxwell, was on a course in St Andrews and could not attend. I drove to St Andrews and persuaded Bargh to sign a letter, drafted by Patrick, allowing Wolfe to attend in his place. It was a good day's work but on the morning of the meeting Russell told me that Maxwell had contacted Milne and told him it had been decided to cancel it. I had a difficult job chasing around the other members assuring them the meeting was in fact still on. Blyth warned me not to persist. Leave Maxwell to get on with running the paper, he said. "Cut out your politicking."

But the meeting was held and they all turned up. An attempt by Goldberg to cancel it, supported by Maxwell and Blyth, was defeated. Then Maxwell objected to the presence of Wolfe who, he said, was a member only of the Investors' Council and had no right to attend. I explained that Wolfe was deputising for Bargh, as permitted by a rule in the Articles. Maxwell continued his protests until I over-ruled them and raised the matter of the price. I had prepared myself well. I circulated a report from Ian Bain showing the effect of the price cut and warned them of their fiduciary duties as directors. With a 5p newspaper we had to increase circulation from 100,000 as it stood, to 517,000 to break even. At the same time, because of a decision by Maxwell to cut advertising rates, we had to increase the advertising content by 25%. I moved formally that the price of the paper should be 6p. Mr Maxwell's reputation, I said, would be at risk but that was not our problem. "A terrible mistake has been made that must inevitably result in the collapse of the paper."

"You don't seem to realise, Allister," said Maxwell in a headmasterly way, "that the problem is one of increasing sales. We must do that to survive. The figures you have quoted, no doubt, are correct. But they are irrelevant."

Wolfe and Milne endorsed my fears but argued that the decision, though fatal, could not be reversed at this stage. Only Russell supported my motion. Our real problem was not the price but Maxwell. I decided to attack the roots.

Maxwell, I said, had assumed dictatorial powers. The price had been reduced without as much as a "by your leave". Nor had the council decided to make him either general manager or company secretary, though he had claimed both posts. "Can we afford to have him much longer?"

Maxwell took up the challenge but was surprisingly mild in his own defence. Blyth and Goldberg jumped to his support. Blyth was particularly vehement.

Wolfe, coming face to face with Maxwell really for the first time, joined the discussion. His approach was forensic – and effective. He relied on the minute-book. A check, he said, showed the only authority vested in Maxwell was in the areas of advertising and circulation. "That being so, why did you then proclaim yourself company secretary and then take on the duties of general manager?"

The question was put quietly. There was no reply. I moved that since it had become evident to all that Maxwell's authority could not be contained he be removed from all executive authority. Russell seconded the motion.

Goldberg launched an attack on me and demanded I resign since

I had lost the confidence of the workforce. Blyth seconded the motion but it was not pursued.

Wolfe intervened again. He feared there could be repercussions among the workforce. We must respect the wishes of the members. He moved the council invest in Maxwell executive powers to deal with circulation and advertising while the other responsibilities of general manager would be handled by myself. Russell persuaded me to drop my motion in favour of Wolfe's which was carried with only three voting against.

Throughout Maxwell had been sitting with quiet dignity, almost as though he were not part of the meeting. But now the councillors had gone too far. They had no right to attempt to restrict his authority. He knew that he could cure the paper's problems, given time. But he had to have the authority. I (Mackie) had from the first said I would not take part in management decisions: in no sense was I management material. He could take no more of the council's floundering. Jumping to his feet, he pointed at Wolfe and Milne, then at me, and, in a mounting hysteria, shouted: "I'll call a mass meeting of this workforce. They'll sort you out."

Russell told him he could not call such a meeting of his own accord.

In a rising pitch Maxwell continued: "I'll be forbidden nothing by the executive council. Nothing, I tell you."

Two days later I received a letter from Wolfe. In it he wrote that he was apprehensive about the future of the company. He did not regard Maxwell's position as being entirely constitutional and regarded his "power leadership within the company as a real threat to the future of the venture." Indeed, he had been astonished by his "childish and extremely unhelpful attitude." He recorded his "extreme disquiet" over the lack of clear and responsible decision-making by the council in respect of Maxwell's responsibilities and of the decision to cut the price of the paper.

ALL OUR energies were now directed at the relaunch. A flop would mean instant death. Each morning Maxwell presided over a management meeting. My own attendance, according to Maxwell, was optional but in my view imperative. Russell asked to attend one morning as a director. In him Maxwell had an implacable enemy. He was cold, impersonal and effective as a rapier. Maxwell feared him and hated him. On Russell's entry to the office, Maxwell stopped in mid-speech and asked him his reasons for being there. Russell smiled amiably and made some comment about wanting to be in at the history-making. Maxwell nodded his head and continued talking.

"Given the amount of advertising I projected you will see that we shall require even less editorial content than we need at present. Let me show you." He produced a 24-page mock-up in the tabloid size. Russell lifted the paste-up and flipped through it. "Tell me, Mr Maxwell, how much advertising are you projecting to the management team? Is it based on likely levels or on your personal promise of bringing in advertisements? There will be a large gap between the two."

Chard, Macgee and Goldberg looked appalled. Douglas Ferguson simply sat and stared at Maxwell, himself harbouring the suspicions that Russell spoke of. Maxwell, sensing the editorial hostility towards Russell, used the situation to reduce the entire struggle to grand farce. Lifting the phone he warned Russell: "If you don't leave immediately I shall at this instant call a mass meeting of the workforce to have you removed from the board."

Russell said or did nothing; he simply smiled at Maxwell's ridiculous postures. Neither would concede and rather than allowing the situation to degenerate to the absurd, I intervened. "Go ahead, Mr Maxwell. Call a mass meeting and let the entire world see how ridiculous you really are."

He slammed the phone down on the cradle and almost as though nothing had happened went on with the meeting completely ignoring Russell's presence.

THE BUILD-UP to the relaunch was an unqualified technical success. During this period I worked occasional shifts in the caseroom. It was not strictly necessary but was done more out of a desire to do something practical. I envied the other compositors their remoteness from commercial realities. I tried to explain them but they preferred not to believe me. My continual repeating of the facts, however, did begin to have an effect.

I was working in the caseroom when an announcement came over the Tannoy. It was Robert Maxwell. We all stopped work not knowing what was coming. The system had been used previously only for emergencies or urgent messages, never as a means of mass communication in the style of Orwell's *1984*. It was a message of encouragement but in it he attacked me because I was telling the membership the effect of the cut in the cover-price. "Set aside Mackie's statements; ignore them. He is not telling the whole story. I give you my assurance that all we need is for a third of the paper to be filled with advertising and I repeat that I can bring all the adverts that you can handle. Already I have secured Government advertising as you will see for yourselves." It was just another lie among a mountain of lies.

The workforce didn't care to listen to the detail. They were developing a blind faith in Maxwell's magic touch. Hadn't he already told a meeting of the FoCs: "Follow Mackie and you are dead; follow Maxwell and you are guaranteed employment forever!"?

CHAPTER TWENTY

Torquemada of the Tannoy

August 15

THE RELAUNCH was a qualified success. Despite Maxwell's instructions to push the print figure to around 500,000, Douglas Ferguson had in his capacity as circulation manager ordered a print of only 240,000. His assessment of demand justified his decision. Although Maxwell and the company claimed that the first three days were a sell-out, I didn't personally believe him and informal reports soon began of thousands of returned copies. And our only chance of survival had been to push the sales to more than 500,000, and that was only to break even. Within the first week it was evident that our last chance had passed us by. Already sales were dwindling to around 200,000, if you could believe Maxwell's claims. (Later, System Three evidence suggested that in fact the sales around that time were probably around 160,000.) Advertising seldom reached 20%, certainly a much lower level than at the launch of the broadsheet three months before. Maxwell's gamble with our newspaper, our savings and our jobs had failed.

Ever since the start of the trouble with Maxwell and the first indications of growing support for him among the workforce, McNamara and I had decided to preserve the records of the struggle, carefully and painstakingly documented by Hooper. One of the first things Maxwell did when he moved into the building on a full-time basis was to ask for the minutes so that the company could commission a history of the co-operative. They were not his property nor that of the company and he had no right to them. Denying all knowledge of their whereabouts to Blyth (who did the inquiring) and Maxwell, I managed to spirit them out of the building, in bits and pieces, with the help of Tommy McGhee, the chief copy telephonist. In addition I carefully collected my own copies of each of the Works Council minutes and at the same time shredded the others, leaving only one set available – my own.

But it was now becoming increasingly difficult to do anything without Maxwell's knowledge. He had taken up residence in the boardroom and nightly made a show of settling down for the night. But really his performance fooled no-one. Almost everybody knew that he had booked a suite at the Albany Hotel and spent the night there after going through the ritual of bedding down. Security men regularly saw him leave by taxi at the main hall, as did many of the others. But it was just one of those small idiosyncrasies that the members could tolerate with a gentle forgiveness: after all he had promised to save all their jobs. What did it matter?

Maxwell's control of the paper inevitably could not be contained to its production. More and more he insisted on making his presence felt on the editorial floor. He started a chat column that proved so disastrous it had to be dropped almost immediately, after protests from the editorial chapel. On another occasion he gave instructions that a story about the inordinate costs of a submarine being fitted out on the Clyde should not be run on the grounds it had been insufficiently checked. The reporter protested. Sillitto dithered. The argument meant the story missed the first edition, when it was discovered that other papers were already running it. The incident cost him a lot of support on the editorial floor.

Even in retrospect I cannot put a coherent interpretation on the events that then ensued. There were so many incidents, so much mental violence, that I felt my life was being scripted for me out of a Kafka novel. It was all related to Maxwell's determination to get rid of me from the chairmanship of the company. I confess even now that I was finding it difficult to think clearly in the environment of harassment. A life-long cultivated sense of direction was my main guiding light. As a youth I had been educated as a Fabian; studied under a working-class educational organisation, the National Council of Labour Colleges; had read socialist literature from Communist Party presses to Socialist Party of Great Britain pamphlets. And the end product of all this was a steel-hard determination to do my own thinking. As I had studied this and that political argument, none of them had totally convinced me; I had to find my own road to socialism or whichever other "ism" led to my concept of the better life. And this was that road now. It mattered less to me that I no longer carried the support of the workforce than the secure knowledge that the direction I was travelling was the correct one. On at least a couple of occasions Goldberg suggested to me that it was time for me to quit and that I had become punch-drunk with all the punishment that had been handed out to me. Blyth joined in with suggestions that the time for fighting against Maxwell was now over and in the interests of the co-operative I ought to accept the realities of that fact.

McNamara, by this time re-elected as FoC of the engineers' chapel, made his contribution to try to help me. It was in the form of a wages demand to Maxwell. It was a justified claim and, in fact, the council had promised months previously to pay the money. But as McNamara saw it, the situation could be used to embarrass Maxwell. This was the flaw in his play. By making his approach to Maxwell, he was by that very fact acknowledging Maxwell's authority, an authority that I was still challenging. Contrary to McNamara's expectations, Maxwell was happy to negotiate and to concede the payment. In all innocence, and guided by the best motives, McNamara had fallen into a trap.

Frequently at this stage when I joined company with friends of many years' standing their conversation would dry up in embarrassment at my presence. But this occurred really only among some compositors. However, as the barriers of estrangement were asserting themselves in some quarters so the bonds of friendship and alliance were growing stronger in the areas where I most sought understanding. There was developing a small but very hard cadre of anti-Maxwell activists. People who had been lying dormant were beginning to show their loyalties quite openly and were discovering the power of those who are in the minority yet know their case to be correct. It was for these people that I held on to office. The temptation of resignation and withdrawal from the struggle was strong and at times almost irresistible. But it was not yet the correct course.

A surprising feature at this time was the absence of physical violence. On one occasion I was approached in the public house, Tom's Bar, by "Stacker" Williamson, a Maxwell devotee who at that time was canvassing for the office of FoC in the Natsopa chapel on the ticket that a "vote for Stacker is a vote for Maxwell". At first he appeared to be genuinely friendly but knowing him of old I suspected his motives. Within seconds he was squaring up aggressively only to discover himself being quickly hustled to the other side of the bar by a phalanx of heavily-built friends of my own, who had been watching his antics. But that incident apart, I do not believe there was any physical violence, which really was quite surprising considering the tension we were all operating in.

At an earlier stage Tough had advised me to take care that my car was not being tampered with, for he believed there was a real threat to my life. At the time I thought it an exaggeration but now I began to reconsider. Patrick, the lawyer, when told of Tough's advice, also advised me to take great care, to check my car before using it and to put the minutes in a safe place in case my house were burgled. I developed the habit, after that conversation, of checking that the brake fluid hadn't been tampered with and that there was nothing attached to the engine that ought not to have been there. In addition, I lied in various quarters, confidentially but in the knowledge that the information would be spread, that the minutes had been safely locked away in the bank. However, this did not mean I could relax. Every time I left home I half expected that the house would be broken into in my absence. The constant vigilance helped to increase the tension and pushed my life almost to a point beyond tolerance.

And then there were the Tannoy harangues. Maxwell would come on and make all sorts of wild accusations and distortions. My own chapel held meetings whose main purpose seemed to be to remove me from the council and put Maxwell indisputably in charge.

It was in this environment of growing tension that I met the members of the Royal Commission on the Press. I did nothing to conceal the state of the company. In their findings they quoted my view that the scope for extending workers' control in the industry as a whole was very limited because the interests of workers and employers were opposed. During the interview with the Commission, a Mrs Anderson said it was a pity that we had not got off the ground more quickly and things would have been more to our advantage if we had. She seemed surprised with my reply.

"I cannot agree. I believe that it was absolutely necessary for us to go through the hardships and the frustrations, because it was just those elements that acted as a mould to cast us into what we became. Crucibles are never pleasant instruments, but they are necessary when you want to harden the metal. Our frustration and hardships, our disappointments and setbacks were our crucible; and they hardened us."

She leaned forward in her seat, smiled with a transparent sympathy, and inquired: "Tell me, Mr Mackie, are you a Calvinist?"

Every thinking Scotsman is a Calvinist; it is part of our heritage. Even Roman Catholics are in some sense Calvinists. It is not a theological point of view, it is an outlook on life. If there is such a thing as a national characteristic, and I believe there is, then a Calvinist outlook is the identifying feature of Scotland and its people. It can be seen in almost every part of our life. Scottish people did not have Calvinism imposed on them by their religion; they imposed Calvinism on their religion. But that is to digress.

BARGH DECIDED to take a hand in trying to save the situation. He knew that the enterprise was dying daily and that one of the factors was the 5p cover price. Outwith my involvement he convened a meeting of the Investors' Council. There was a full turn-out – Bargh, Wolfe, Milne, Canavan, Russell and myself. The meeting simply looked at the financial position, accepted the inevitable solution of increasing the price as soon as possible, and that was that. Within a few days as company chairman, I received a letter from Bargh officially setting this out as the view of the council.

The stage was now set for the next meeting of the Works Council, due to be held on September 1. We all knew it was going to be a crunch meeting. There was no sign of the miracle that Maxwell had promised everyone. It was true that the contents of the paper, though erratic, were showing distinct signs of improvement. But the sales were continuing their downward course and advertising was disappearing just as quickly. So much for the boasts of "so much advertising that we wouldn't be able to cope with it". We actually had much less advertising income at this stage, with Maxwell in control, than we enjoyed at the start.

September 1

WOLFE TURNED up for the meeting, this time to represent Jimmy Milne. Maxwell was not there, with no apology or reason for his absence. The first task was to find a company secretary. Russell proposed Wolfe and to my surprise but inestimable relief he accepted. There was no vote.

Rankine Durnin was acting as our third financial controller in four months. He was, as Tough had been, seconded from PA. In his report he told us of the company's worsening financial state. After two weeks of the relaunched tabloid, we were losing more than £20,000 a week, and that was putting an optimistic interpretation on the sales returns. He advised us that we could not survive for more than 10 weeks and that we might soon be in contravention of the Companies Act, which said we could not continue trading unless we had a foreseeable future. "Unless in the near future we can prove that we can reasonably hope to return to a profitable situation, we must call in a voluntary liquidator who will do what he must either to save the company or wind it up. The choice is not an easy one but it must be looked at soon." We had been briefed about the Act on occasions before. But the advice when it came was a shocker.

Blyth gave a brief report on the findings of the latest System Three report. It looked encouraging. It wasn't yet time for dying: we agreed to fight on. But we had to make the absolutely correct decisions if we were to survive. The need to increase the price of the paper to 6p was becoming more necessary by the minute. There could be no question of delaying it any further. With the increase we could survive perhaps for another two or three weeks, perhaps long enough to allow us to appeal to the public for support. I argued that our tactics must still be to remove Maxwell, show the public the effect he had had on the viability of the company, then appeal to their sympathy and ask them to rally behind us. I did not make the proposal simply for the purpose of getting at Maxwell. To me it was the correct commercial decision. Indeed I was prepared to put the price up to 7p and back it up with a massive trade union appeal for support. To this day I believe that survival would have been more likely had we taken the plunge. But there was little support for my extreme measures. In the end the council agreed to increase the price of the paper to 6p on September 22, in three weeks' time, and to observe secrecy so that there would be no adverse press comment from other newspapers who were smelling out our crisis.

To add to our burden, Beaverbrook let us know that unless they received a cheque for the £59,000 due to them within 24 hours they intended issuing a writ against us. It would have destroyed our credibility overnight and almost certainly have precipitated the company's collapse. After a call to Tony Dyer in the *Express* building in Fleet Street I succeeded in persuading him to call off the legal eagles and allow us to discuss the position in a more reasonable calm. The council members then decided to go against Maxwell's handling of the transaction and to pay the money. After all, it was felt, it was Beaverbrook's in the first place. We had no legal right to it at all. Winding up the meeting, I reminded the members that it was Maxwell who had been the cause of most of the problems discussed that afternoon and that therefore it was my intention at the next meeting of the council, to be held in a few days' time, to seek his removal once again from executive authority in the company.

When everyone had gone Russell and I were left discussing the situation. He felt, as I probably did myself, that my warning about my intention to remove Maxwell was possibly a bad tactic: it would give him time to retaliate.

As we spoke Russell was leafing through the System Three report which had been delivered by Blyth just before the meeting. Blyth had referred to it at the meeting, quoting how it had shown that the paper was holding its own. But this was not what we read as we began to analyse the report. It showed that the original sales had never been 240,000; in fact it was optimistic to claim they were in excess of 180,000. And the present sales, far from being the 200,000 claimed by Maxwell, were in the region of 130,000. If the report were accurate, there could be no hope of survival: we were already finished. Why had Blyth put so different a gloss on the report? He was in the outer office speaking to "Magic" Miller about some publicity arrangements.

"Maxwell told me what the results were: I never really studied the figures myself. Are they really that bad?" he asked.

They were bad enough, I replied. But we would get Douglas Ferguson and his reps to do a random check over as much of Scotland as we could manage in a couple of days. "But, mark you, if it shows up the same result, we're in dead trouble." Blyth pondered for a moment and then walked off.

We failed yet again to anticipate quite how Maxwell would fight back and just how dirty the fight would become. Two nights later the by now regular broadcast came over the Tannoy:

"Attention. This is Robert Maxwell speaking. We have doubled our circulation. What a time to pick by these terrible people, the enemy in our midst, to destroy our courage and our reputation. I want you to reflect carefully on what I have said. Now is the time that you have to stand up and make up your mind – either you want the management and leadership I have provided or else you can take the situation which Mackie and Russell and their like have brought about.

"The DTI has asked me to go to a meeting on Tuesday. I can't go to that meeting with a divided voice. I think you ought to know that Mr Mackie, without notice to me, has taken the decision to increase the price of our newspaper to 6p as from September 21. This increase would be suicidal to our credit and livelihood.

"I have held up a cheque for £59,000 to Beaverbrook because they have not fulfilled their promise on machinery. In addition, Beaverbrook owe this company £40,000. Mackie insists that it be sent and signed the cheque without my permission. I am sorry to give you this dreadful news. This is Mackie and Russell for reasons of their own who wish to play politics with the safety of your jobs. Now is the time to let your feelings be known. I have ordered the caseroom management to tell Allister Mackie that he should do a full day's work for the money he gets. It is therefore up to you. I want to hear from your chapel representatives what you want to do to save your jobs. Thanks and good night."

On that evening, ever mindful of Maxwell's whims, the caseroom chapel passed a vote of no confidence in myself. The following day Alex Munro, the head printer, dutifully took it on himself to advise me to return to work in the caseroom. To his credit he was embarrassed and showed no love for his task.

The broadcasts were becoming more and more frequent and were more and more violent in their content. Of all the iniquities heaped on me by Maxwell, I believe that the Tannoy broadcasts were the most damaging to my mind. He would have put Torquemada to shame. I would lie in bed at night and hear the booming tones of the tyrant as he practised the role of torturer. His reign of terror knew no limits. He completely ignored the System Three report and would not discuss it in depth either with the council or the management teams. He insisted that the company was in a healthy state and that my prognostications of gloom were totally unfounded. This had the management team at sixes and sevens. I suspect they believed me but preferred to listen to Maxwell. Certainly they worried me when they continued acquiring creditors at a time when they must have known there was very little chance of paying off their debts; it was immoral. On one occasion we were discussing taking on advertising space with a firm which had started advertising on public buses. The chances of this firm ever getting money out of us were remote and I knew this. I tried to warn the director we discussed the business with but he didn't seem to read my language. In the end he went ahead and signed us up for a considerable contract. As it turned out he was one of the lucky ones who was paid. But there must have been many more who lost.

CHAPTER TWENTY-ONE

Learning how to die

September 3

ON SEPTEMBER 3 there was another council meeting. This time
Maxwell made a point of being there. Wolfe attended for the first time
in the capacity of company secretary. Maxwell lost no time in
confronting Bargh and Milne. By what right had the Investors'
Council discussed the company's business in general and the price of
the paper in particular, he asked.

Milne, his high-pitched Aberdonian voice charged with
controlled emotion, squared his shoulders as he addressed Maxwell. If
the Investors' Council thought Maxwell's stewardship of the company
was damaging the interests of investors, then the council not only had
the right but the responsibility to make its voice heard.

"You offered no help when the paper was sliding," said Maxwell.
"Why do you interfere now?"

Goldberg spoke in support of Maxwell and then Bargh entered
the fray. When Maxwell unilaterally made decisions like changing the
price of the paper and prejudicing the interests of the investors, then
they had a responsibility to record their protest.

Maxwell then turned to the cheque for Beaverbrook. "I know
what you decided in my absence at the last meeting but I am
informing you all here and now that I have held up the cheque.
They're not getting a brown penny from us and that's final. Well, at
least not until they cough up the £40,000 they owe us."

Patrick pointed out that there was no legal claim on Beaverbrook
for that money. The two payments were in no way related and had to
be considered separately.

Milne proposed a compromise – that the money should be placed in the hands of an auditor of the court thus indicating our willingness and ability to pay the money. Maxwell accepted the idea with alacrity. He called it "excellent". Now he moved on to his progress report. It too was "excellent".

I looked over to him in wonderment. How could he possibly speak of excellent reports when surely he realised that the company was bleeding to death, its resources haemorrhaging. But we all want to believe in miracles, and so I waited.

"I have made a major breakthrough in advertising," said Maxwell. He paused and looked around the large walnut table as though waiting for applause. He lifted his briefcase and started to fumble among the contents. At last he found what he was looking for and with a smile tossed a letter on the table.

"That is what I can do to help the paper. This is what I mean when I tell you that you need someone of my standing to direct its affairs. I have this letter from a major advertiser who is committing his company to advertising with the *News*."

I lifted the letter and started to read it. The letter was signed by David Jones, publicity director of EMI Cinemas. It said that he had persuaded the local management to advertise the three city-centre and seven suburban cinemas each Friday, at a discount of 40% on normal rates. The advertisements were to be 9cm single-column and 8cm respectively. He had also advised the distributors to reserve display space whenever possible on the company's releases in Glasgow.

"Is this your excellent report?" I asked. "A couple of piddling single-column ads is all that this letter offers." What was more, I went on, I knew for certain that the deal had already been negotiated by June Murdoch, one of our sales reps, weeks before. It had been only a matter of time before EMI would have taken the space. "Now you are claiming her work and you are offering a discount of 40% which wasn't necessary. What game are you playing at? Are you trying to ruin the company?"

He was seated at the opposite end of the long table. I have never seen eyes so charged with hate. Jumping to his feet he grabbed his pile of correspondence, spilling some in his temper, and shouted: "You'll never get anywhere so long as Mackie's in that chair. You've all seen for yourself the sort of encouragement I get from him." Muttering inarticulately, he stormed from the room.

However, before long he returned, to be informed that in his absence the other members of the council had agreed unanimously that the price of the paper would have to be restored to 6p by the end of September. He agreed with the decision.

Russell tackled him about the Tannoy message in which both he and I had been slandered. He paused, as if wondering which specific message Russell was referring to. "Oh, that broadcast," he eventually said. He explained it had been based on information given him by Blyth. "Sorry. It won't happen again." But the broadcasts became more and more frequent.

The question of the Beaverbrook money became more and more curious as the days passed. Patrick, after careful study, advised that in fact Beaverbrook had had no legal claim on it until Maxwell, in a letter to Tony Dyer of Beaverbrook, had used the phrase "I will not release the cheque for £59,000 *due* to your company . . . " So much for Maxwell's business acumen. It had scored brilliantly for us once again! That little three-lettered word cost us endless debate and eventually our credit.

EVEN AT this late stage of our relationship, marked as it was by mistrust and, I suppose, fear, Maxwell still tried to woo my support. One day we were seated at his desk with perhaps five minutes to spare. We were at moments like these perfectly civil to each other and capable of communicating at a personal level. On this occasion he tapped my hand and looked at me with an apparent earnestness.

"Allister, why do you always try to hurt me? Why do you always mistrust me? Don't you realise that I am just like other men? When I am pricked do I not bleed?"

He had a habit of speaking with his eyes, a habit I tend to loathe in men.

"For God's sake, don't give me the Shylock routine. You know what is the score between us. I don't waste my time hating you. What I hate is what you are trying to do to the workforce. Already you have corrupted them and they deserve a far better fate than that. The way you have perverted our members is your biggest crime."

The remaining days were spent in an agony of apprehension.

There was no longer even a slight chance of survival. The last desperate option by this time, as I saw it, was to throw Maxwell out of office and increase the price of the paper to 7p, at the same time making a massive appeal to the public and unions to give us another chance. If it was necessary for the survival of the co-operative I was willing to assassinate Maxwell's image by public exposure. But by this time there were very few of us willing to fight Maxwell "to the death". Russell was one of the very few and he was going off to Italy for a fortnight's holiday. This left me with a terrible sense of isolation. A few others stood by but increasingly we accepted there was now very little hope of saving the paper and were willing to admit it. At home I was beginning to receive phone calls from irate wives demanding that I hand over complete control to Maxwell and stop all the fighting that was bleeding the paper to death. Even some of my dearest friends were turning on me like a pack of wolves. It was sad to witness the mistrust and lack of sympathy and understanding. Yet another source of annoyance was when "interested" shareholders would phone up at 6.30am to inquire about the security of their investment. They would seldom offer their names and I suspected it was just part of a campaign to sicken me. But it was not yet time for resigning.

I had discussed the situation fully with Alex Ferry, the local organiser of the AUEW. What he was most concerned about was not myself, because that's apparently how you learn to accept things in the unions, but what effect the whole struggle would have on the Labour Movement. It was essential that the co-operative should not be seen to have failed. There would be others in the future and their coming should not be aborted by our failure. Maxwell would have to be seen to destroy me before I resigned, otherwise we might have been accused of running away. Ferry's formula we eventually accepted as the best in the interests of the Labour Movement. All that was required was the occasion, and that did not seem to be far off. I suspect I accepted his proposal because I knew of no other way to resign.

September 12

ONLY A couple of days after meeting Ferry, I was phoned by Patrick who asked me to come over to his office for a discussion on the state of the company. Milne and Wolfe would be there. Legal requirements had to be met. I knew what he meant.

Patrick was in a state of anxious impatience when I arrived. Once we were assembled, Patrick, Wolfe, Milne, Dallas and I, he went straight down to business. Patrick informed us as our legal adviser that the time had come to call in the liquidator. Patrick added: "As company chairman, you have a personal responsibility, Allister."

He looked at me, his eyes almost awash with a great sadness and continued: "I'm sorry. There's no alternative. It's got to be done here and now." We were losing cash at a rate that could not possibly justify our continuing in office as directors. We had responsibility under the Companies Act to shareholders and creditors.

I looked round the room at my friends. Milne was used to taking hard decisions. He showed few signs of emotion. Wolfe had been through it all before in his own life but, having the heart of a giant, was suffering pangs along with me. And Dallas sat unblinking. I knew what he felt: we had travelled a long, hard and strange journey together.

"All right then. Let's prepare for the death. What's to be done?"

I thought of Christmas two years before when my wife was expecting our first child. As we travelled between Linlithgow and Bathgate, my wife and a friend, both Catholics, started to sing a Catholic hymn. It was about St Joseph and the last line excited me. I remembered the occasion clearly; we were passing through the village of Torphichen at the time, the birthplace of Lord Beaverbrook's father and the home of Wolfe. The words ran: "Teach us, teach us how to die."

At the time they sounded pensive, full of meaning. They must have been written by one who had known the meaning of suffering. They came back to me in their full force now. How should we die? Was it to be in a clean, dignified working-class manner, as McNamara wished? Or would it be a cut-throat episode with Maxwell leading the workers like a brigand chief? I prayed for the former and feared the latter. We had fought and failed. There is no loss of dignity in defeat. And dignity was the only consolation we could hope to salvage from the disaster.

Wolfe was being given instructions, as company secretary, to prepare for the council a liquidation document. He wasted no time.

With the help of Dallas he got right down to the painful business and drew out a rough copy. After a few amendments it was finalised. It is reproduced at the end of the book as an appendix.

I read it over. It showed an estimated deficiency of £724,500. I noted the appeal to the Government for help. We could use it at a meeting we were to have with Bruce Millan the next day. Bargh and Maxwell were to be there too.

I left the lawyer's office with a heavy heart. Until the moment he had spelled out the situation and what we must do there had been always hope. Now even that was behind me. Life seemed to be an endless procession of disappointments, a road littered with decomposing hopes.

IN ALBION STREET I showed a copy of the report to Blyth, Goldberg and Lindsay. I located Russell in Italy by phone and he agreed that the lawyer's advice to put the company into liquidation should be followed.

On the Saturday afternoon I was surprised to find Sillitto and Blyth waiting for me at the office. Bargh was also there and I showed him the statement by Wolfe. He read it through carefully, asked a couple of questions, and then nodded his head in agreement. He was a nice, friendly gem of a man, with a good understanding born of long experience.

Maxwell arrived, dressed in a polo-necked sweater. I showed him a copy of the report. "Yes, I know about it," he said. "Blyth has already told me." But he took his copy and quickly scanned it.

When it was time to go to the meeting at the Department of Trade offices in St Vincent Street, Blyth and Sillitto presented themselves. Maxwell said; "I'm sure you won't mind them coming along. I thought they might just add a little weight to the delegation."

I raised no objections. On the way I gave Sillitto his copy of the Wolfe report. Until that moment I had forgotten that he was actually still a member of the council. Yet here he was "adding weight" to the delegation.

As we waited in an ante-room for the Minister's arrival, I outlined how the meeting was to be conducted. I would open and appeal for more Government help, using Wolfe's report. "It's best to be totally honest with Millan. He knows the score anyway and it will give him the way for the Government to help."

Maxwell began to question the wisdom of using the report, but consented at the last second as we were ushered into the meeting room where we sat at an oval table, with Millan sat opposite me flanked by his civil servants. These men were no automatons. They had sincerely wished us well and I believe would have given their all to help us further. Bargh sat on my immediate right, with Blyth and Sillitto to my left. Maxwell had positioned himself at the right of Bargh, right on the corner, so that he was at right angles almost to Millan and myself.

After the usual formalities I showed Millan the Wolfe report. He was half way through reading the part where Wolfe was proposing Government help when Maxwell interrupted.

"Mr Minister," he said, "I must ask you not to give any consideration to that report. The chairman had no right to give it to you, since it has not yet been passed by the board. In addition, it has been prepared by an enemy of the co-operative who is working in the interests of our biggest competitor, Sir Hugh Fraser." By this time his voice was becoming louder and louder.

Millan didn't bat an eyelid. He simply looked at Maxwell, glanced over to me with a bland expression, handed me back the document, then turned to ask Maxwell what steps, if any, the Government could take to help.

Before Maxwell could speak, however, I apologised to Millan for Maxwell's abominable behaviour and asked him to discount his "rantings". He was not speaking for the delegation and his views were personal. It was the first meeting that Maxwell had attended with a Minister on behalf of the *News*. And he had behaved like a street brawler.

There was little return from that meeting. And little wonder. If we behaved like that in front of a Government Minister what chance could we ever have of receiving further help? We didn't deserve any.

After the meeting, back in the street, I demanded an apology from Maxwell. He stood staring at me in wonderment for a few moments, his polo-necked sweater and cloth cap making him look slightly incongruous for a millionaire. Then he exploded. "Apologise? We'll see what the workforce say by way of apologies. I'll take this to the workforce. Just you wait."

And he did. On the Sunday evening he made yet another Tannoy broadcast. But on this occasion few people knew what his message was. He worked himself into a state of frantic hysteria. He huffed and raved without pause. Later no-one could tell me what he said, but everyone agreed that it was one of the most frightening experiences of their lives. In the editorial floor he was openly booed by some of the now disenchanted journalists, while another journalist tried in vain to cut off the Tannoy system completely. Only one part of his message was understood. There was to be a mass meeting of the workforce the following day at noon; and that Mackie had tried to put the company into liquidation.

The first I heard of the meeting was when McNamara phoned me up after the broadcast. "He's now completely off his nut, Allister, you should have heard him." He added: "This is it, Al. He'll take control tomorrow. There's no doubt about it and nothing is going to stop him."

No-one else phoned that night. In the morning Crossan gave me a ring to confirm the meeting was on. Would I be attending? It was difficult for me. I was due to be at a District Council meeting that morning and it was almost impossible to opt out at that late stage. And anyway, as I reasoned, this is the moment I had been waiting for. If Maxwell destroyed me, to the extent that I was forced to resign, I could then put into effect the Ferry plan. I would have to wait quietly though my nerves were beginning to react to the hammerings they were taking.

We had had our fight – and now it was almost over. The experience had been fantastic and all that it had really cost me was money. Not much money, just all of it. My return had been the experience and the education. There were few regrets. My motives had always been correct. But for the present my life was a terribly lonely place. No-one could share it with me.

CHAPTER TWENTY-TWO

Bucketfuls of blood

September 15

MAXWELL HAD prepared for the mass meeting by circulating a letter to the workforce. It falsely claimed that our circulation and advertising revenue had more than doubled. Our losses, which had been running well in excess of £30,000, would reduce that week to about £17,000. The company was fully solvent and heading towards break-even. The attempt by Mr Wolfe, Mr Mackie, Mr Russell, Mr McNamara and some others to push it into liquidation was "as unnecessary as it is despicable." If these irresponsible elements were allowed to continue in authority then the only result would be closure and the loss of jobs. He was sure that "you will no longer tolerate anyone in our midst playing politics or irresponsible games with the security of our paper and its 500 jobs". At the meeting the workforce had to decide whether they would clear out those people in favour of liquidation and give their authority to those members of the Executive Council who were against it: Mr A. Blyth, Mr N. Goldberg, Mr R. Maxwell, Mr F. Sillitto.

"If that is your decision then I assure you we will have no difficulty in preventing this calamity."

Finally, *because* of Mr Wolfe's "alarmist" statement, together with Mr Mackie's and Mr Russell's support of it, it was clear the company would need a cash injection of the order of £200,000. "I am prepared to make a contribution of additional capital and know that others are also prepared to do so. Many members of the workforce have intimated to me that they themselves would be prepared to make some additional investment as a way of securing that the paper is given a fair chance of success." He concluded that he was optimistic that they would have no difficulty in getting support from the Government and other sources.

I knew nothing of the letter as I entered the building or of Maxwell's campaign of lies and half-truths that had been carried out on the previous evening. He had gone round various chapels telling them that I was determined to close the paper down, that it was in a healthy state and that Wolfe had already prepared a liquidation document. In fact he showed them a part of the document but not that which contained the appeal for Government assistance. Wolfe was again projected as an enemy of the co-operative. Blyth and Sillitto, though they had attended the meeting on the Saturday and knew the whole picture, did nothing to save the reputation of one of the co-operative's closest and most loyal allies.

This was the background to the meeting as I arrived on the editorial floor at 12.30pm. I don't think Maxwell expected me to turn up. Certainly Alex Munro, who was chairing the meeting in my place, was a picture of embarrassment as I approached the table. At first there was a hush, then one or two members made a timorous booing noise. There was no point in wasting any time. Without ceremony I commanded the floor.

"I don't know what Mr Maxwell has already told you. But I will guarantee that he has been feeding all of you on a diet of lies about the state of the company and the part that the Works Council, including myself, has played in it. The position is this. We do not have enough cash to pay out wages for more than four weeks, pay off our creditors, and set aside a sum you are entitled to in lieu of holiday wages. We are told by our lawyers that at this moment we are in breach of the law if we continue trading. We have never broken the law, we were always very careful not to.

"I accept that what I am telling you is probably different from the picture that Maxwell paints. But the difference is that I am telling you the truth, just as I always have. And you have a responsibility to face the truth when it stares you in the face. It may be that you have already agreed to have me removed. If so then I can tell you to forget it. This is not a constitutional meeting. It has no rights, and the Council will not, on my advice, give it any credence.

"Finally I make it clear to you. If you decide that you want to hand over control of the co-operative to Maxwell, and I suspect that this is the reason why Maxwell called the meeting, so that you will do so, then not only must you accept Maxwell's techniques of management, you must also accept his level of morality with it. And I fear that that may be a bit too much for many of you to stomach."

Maxwell's sole defence was simply to repeat that there was no crisis and that I was misleading the members since it was not legally incumbent on a company when going into liquidation to make provision for holiday payments.

I made to leave but Macgee demanded to know if it were true that liquidation had been discussed at any stage.

"I have already told you that we have been advised by our lawyers to look at the question of liquidation. It is a legal requirement and no amount of words from Maxwell can alter that situation. Yes, liquidation has been looked at. But no decision has been made."

With that I left. There was an embarrassed hush but no evidence of personal hostility. I believe that most members knew I was being painfully truthful and consciences were being sorely tried. When I had taken only a few steps from the table, Maxwell tried to lead the meeting into booing me out of the door. I stopped to turn round and take a look at the tired, pathetic figure introducing his new style of leadership. No-one joined him in his futile tantrums.

After my departure the meeting continued, but with a deep restraint. Maxwell made them commit one half of a week's wages every month to buy more worthless shares. It was an act that was irresponsible in the worst way. It simply meant that the winding-up would be costly as well as painful for them.

In the end the meeting had a resolution put to it from the caseroom chapel, composed mainly by the pen of Grant, the head reader, the same one who had longed for a taste of the master's whip. It read:

> At a recent SGA (Scottish Graphical Association) Chapel meeting we expressed our confidence in Robert Maxwell's proven economic expertise to guide and assist our enterprise. In view of the repeating pattern of events which occur in the Works Council in Robert Maxwell's absence, this SGA Chapel records a vote of no confidence in Allister Mackie's continuance as chairman and

> invites him accordingly to resign at this stage and seek re-election.
> This meeting today endorses the SGA motion and also expresses a
> vote of no-confidence in W. Wolfe's position as secretary and
> invites them to resign their positions and if they wish they can
> stand for re-election at a meeting to be convened at a later date.

This resolution, which came from a chapel that I had been a member of
for 14 years and that I had served to my ability as FoC, was put to the
vote. There was massive support for it. But this was not enough for
Maxwell. When he was looking for blood he demanded bucketfuls of
it. He insisted that the attendance and the vote be counted. It turned
out to be: For, 312; Against, 12 (thereafter referred to as the Dirty
Dozen); Abstentions, 13.

The question of further contributions from the membership was
put to a vote and was carried with around the same majority. No-one
thought to remind Maxwell of the extra capital he had promised them.
And certainly he made no reference to it or the mountains of
advertising that we wouldn't be able to handle.

At the meeting of the council on the same afternoon I chaired the
meeting for the last time. Even then, Maxwell's appetite was not
satisfied. He had prepared letters for Wolfe and me. The letter to Wolfe
denounced his unwarranted action which unnecessarily endangered the
News, expressed disgust at his "unprofessional conduct" and added: "For
a public figure who is the chairman of the Scottish Nationalist (*sic*) Party
your callous conduct in jeopardising the livelihood of 500 men and the
existence of a new and important national newspaper will no doubt be
noted by your members and the public at large."

My billet-doux took the form of an internal memo. Compared
with the letter to Wolfe, it was relatively restrained, denouncing my
decision to show the Wolfe report to Millan and to repay the money
to Beaverbrook.

Neither of us showed any reaction as he handed them to us. By
this time we had become immune to further attacks. Thank God, the
fighting was over. All that was left for me to do was to retreat in a
civilised manner. I made it clear that I accepted no recommendations
from the mass meeting of that morning. It had been unconstitutional,
without authority.

"Nonetheless I cannot ignore the feelings of the membership . . .
I now believe that the membership sincerely wish to wind up the co-

operative and hand over control of the company to Robert Maxwell. I will not stand in their way. But I shall not serve in any executive capacity in a company that is controlled by Robert Maxwell. Accordingly I tender my resignation as chairman of the company and as a member of the council."

I felt very little sadness at that moment, only an overwhelming sense of relief. The weight of responsibility that I had been carrying had been increasing daily until it had become intolerable. I confess that I tried to appear in a mood of dejection or sadness but it was not there. A tide of strange, inexplicable well-being seemed to take over, the sensation that although all around is in ruin the world is beautiful. Perhaps it is nature's way of protecting you from the reality of a disaster. It may simply be a sense of gratitude that despite all else you have survived.

Wolfe followed with a prepared statement. He had done his duty with a clear conscience and was not prepared to prevaricate and disguise the seriousness of the financial situation, or to hide it from the Executive Council.

"I note that the workforce believes that Robert Maxwell can keep the company going. I hope their confidence is fulfilled. I resign in order to leave him to operate as he sees fit."

Patrick now made Boyd's legal position quite clear. "We accept no legal responsibility for the company from now on. I advise you as directors that you have legal responsibilities under Section 332 of the Companies Act. If you are not willing to accept these responsibilities then you have a clear duty to resign."

Briston, who had remained quiet up to this point, observing the carnage around him, spoke up: "I am to inform you that as from this moment James Russell resigns as a member of the Works Council. I have from him here a letter which authorises me to make this announcement."

And that was it. In my interview with the press I again stressed that my reason for resigning was the decision of the workforce to hand over control to Maxwell and that it was therefore no longer a co-operative. One of the reporters, on being told that Maxwell had appointed Blyth as chairman in my place, asked me to confirm the difference in the spelling of our Christian names.

"Alister Blyth spells his name with one *l*, and I with two. And as you are all aware there is one *l* of a difference between us."

Apart from Blyth, Maxwell appointed Dorothy Grace Elder and Tom Clarke a member of the NATSOPA chapel as members of the council in place of Russell and myself. Maxwell also appointed Goldberg editor over Sillitto, which was not too bad a move but a bit surprising.

But Maxwell being Maxwell could not leave the editorial content solely to Goldberg's discretion. He took it on himself to send a memo to all the senior editorial staff instructing them to change the editorial style of the paper. In his view the paper was too serious and the editor was told to "go for stories which can help advertising and circulation." Goldberg seemed not to have read Maxwell's edict or, alternatively, chose to ignore it. In fact little changed other than a general improvement in content and design due, I believe, to Goldberg's personal contribution.

The paper limped on, staggering from one crisis to the next. Within a few days Beaverbrook issued their threatened writ for £59,000. The paper's credit dried up almost overnight. After a break of two weeks I returned to work in the caseroom. It was not an easy decision, and it had taken the entire two weeks to make it. My first reaction had been to look for another job. But I couldn't make the break. I still felt committed to help the workforce. I still had the responsibility of making sure that we "wound up in a proper working-class manner", whatever that meant.

The size of the vote against me had had little impact on my ego. At times I fear that it is beyond damage or destruction. On one occasion in the old days of the *Express* caseroom I had been defeated on a vital issue by a majority of 118-1. Even on that occasion it had never occurred to me that I may have been wrong: what surprised me about the vote was that so many people could make the same mistake at the same time.

My return to the tools was a bit uncomfortable for me but much more uncomfortable for those there who had led the campaign against me. Now their cry was one of "we didn't know the facts" as the sales continued to disappear and the mountains of Maxwell's advertising still failed to show up.

Gilbert Smith, an honest person and one of the caseroom staff who had made a last-minute switch to Maxwell, explained his reasons to me: "We honestly believed that all you were after was to stay in office as chairman, and that the state of the company was incidental to you. That was the reason so many of us turned against you."

"But surely if I only wanted to remain in office all I had to do was to support Maxwell. There would have been no problem then."

His look of enlightenment gave way to one of embarrassment. "I'm sorry, Allister. You're right. But we didn't see it that way at the time. Maxwell made it look different."

On the Wednesday after my return a mass meeting was held on the editorial floor. I again offered my services to approach the Government for help, but with the prerequisite that Maxwell be removed from the company. The proposal was not so readily dismissed as I had expected but with the chair and the entire council in the Maxwell camp there could be no change of direction.

It is not possible to catalogue with clarity the events that held us together as captives over the following days. The company reeled from one crisis to the next with a sense of neither direction nor purpose. We were doomed and we all now knew it. All other options by this time had been eliminated. Most of us simply carried on with our work accepting our fates with a curious stoicism that compelled us to hang around for the funeral.

But even in those latter days of the *News* Maxwell still held many of the workforce in his spell. To add to our already intolerable sense of frustration, they argued that the demise of the paper was all part of a Maxwell 'grand strategy' – that immediately after the closure of the paper he intended to start up another with a carefully chosen staff and from the same building. All they needed to secure their personal futures was to keep alive their faith in their messiah and their loyalty was sure to be rewarded.

October 2

AT THIS stage mass meetings were being held with an almost monotonous regularity – at least once a week. Their main purpose seemed to be to prop up the tottering faith the workforce had in its own future. But facts are chiels that cannot be denied – print figures were being maintained but unsold returns were on the increase and there was still no indications of improved advertising. It was in this environment of resigned despair a meeting was held on October 2. It was held a few days after a two-page article appeared in the *Sunday Times* condemning Maxwell for raping our ideal of co-operative. It was undoubtedly a damning indictment of Maxwell's conduct but in my view was based totally on proven fact and rational conclusion. Maxwell offered a feeble defence of himself and criticised the authors of the article and then shook us all by his winding up: "As a consequence of the bad publicity I feel I can no longer continue to be involved with the company. My personal credibility has been so badly damaged that I can no longer be of service to you." All this only three weeks after he had brought about my own resignation.

Many of us pointed out that it was not the *Sunday Times* article which had damaged his credibility but his own actions since everything in the article had been correct. Others joined in as the hostility to Maxwell mounted. Journalists, now among his fiercest opponents, engineers and even compositors were criticising his performance. Maxwell tried to end the baiting.

"Undoubtedly the most hurtful of all the lies told about me in the *Sunday Times* article was the final paragraph where Mackie accused me of being a fascist. Allister, as you know I am no fascist. Won't you recant that part of the article?"

I was amazed. Here he was after doing everything he could to assassinate my character, asking for sympathy. He was out of luck. I felt sorry for him but the members had to be made aware of what they had done.

"There is nothing I will recant in my statement either to the press or to yourself. At the time I made the statement that you were a fascist it was done because I sincerely believed you were one. But I admit that at that time there wasn't all that much you had done to earn the comment. You have since. You have come to power through terror, repression, lies, half-truths, deceits, false promises and control of the Tannoy system in the building. Exactly the methods employed by Hitler in the 1930s. Indeed, your broadcasts were very similar to Hitler's rantings at Nuremberg. In relation to yourself I recant nothing and I regret nothing."

I have never seen a man quite so defeated. He sat with his head hung, wiping moisture from his eyes, and made no defence of himself. He was pathetic to look at. I have been beaten often before and many defeats lie waiting for me in the future; but I have never been broken with defeat. But Maxwell had the appearance of a completely broken man. Hatred is an emotion that is entirely alien to me. There are those in life whom I love less than others, and dislike myself for it. I find life easier to live this way, since it is easier to live with a friend than with an enemy. At that moment of bitterness I felt a strong compassion for Robert Maxwell. He was a man who believed that power and money could buy happiness, yet having both he was still a desperately unhappy man. We all look for happiness. Sometimes we look for it in religion, or in money or power. Sometimes we find it in love while others confuse their goal with pleasure. But it is the grand illusion of happiness that we all chase after. Maxwell, in that sense, was no different from the rest of us. He was only looking for it in the wrong place and at the same time was prepared to pay too high a price for it.

A WEEK after Maxwell's flight south the council called in the liquidator. At a mass meeting called the week after his appointment he admitted that had he been called in six weeks earlier he could have done something to save the paper. Now it was too late. The following week Whitten, the liquidator, was giving his report to the workforce advising us that there were only two weeks' wages left. He then fished around an inside pocket and withdrew a folded letter. "I must advise you that I have received a bid from Mr Maxwell; he wants to buy the building and plant for £650,000. Of course I have refused the offer."

There was a spontaneous catcalling and derisory hooting from the gathered members. But still his acolytes on the Works Council paid homage to their absent master. Following the meeting one of the switchboard operators accidentally intercepted a phone call from Maxwell to Goldberg in which Maxwell asked if his bid had been announced and what had been the workforce's reaction; and then finished off by instructing Goldberg to prepare a press release with the details of the bid.

At this meeting I proposed that as a last desperate gesture we should go out fighting by publicly dissociating ourselves from Robert Maxwell and re-declaring our faith in the co-operative at the same time appealing to the public, trade union movement and the Government for help. I believe the bulk of our members supported my proposal but the hand-picked Works Council, perhaps still believing in the Maxwell 'grand strategy', would not be associated with any statement critical of Maxwell, and thus ended the final death throe.

Freed from the constraints of Sillitto's inborn sense of perspective and caution, the contents of the paper deteriorated rapidly in its content. From being an organ of news dissemination it rapidly degenerated into an organ campaigning for its own survival with the leaders almost imposing a sense of guilt on its readers for not having done more to save the *News*.

In the final few days I was asked to join the campaign committee to save the *News*. I refused. The time had come for dying. In the last forty-eight hours I helped along with Crossan, McNamara, Bob Mackay, an electrician, and McAskill, to make sure that there would be no vandalism. Chapel volunteers policed the building but their presence proved unnecessary. The paper that had been born a co-operative died in quiet working-class dignity, just as McNamara wished.

APPENDIX

SCOTTISH NEWS ENTERPRISES LTD

Report to Chairman and members of the Executive Council by William Wolfe, Company Secretary, 13th September 1975.

1. The Acting Financial Controller of the Company has drawn up a Trading and Profit and Loss Account for the period to 23rd August 1975 and a provisional Balance Sheet as at that date, and has made estimates of the position as at 13th September 1975. His letter to me reporting on these provisional accounts is appended to this Report.

2. These provisional accounts show that the position of the Company on 13th September was extremely bad, but as they are based on book values it is essential for the Directors to examine the situation on the basis of realisable values.

3. It is quite clear from the provisional accounts that the rate of loss-making (currently estimated at £20,000 per week) is such that the Directors must take immediate action to try and safeguard the interests of Creditors, quite apart from what the net resources of the Company might be at the present time.

4. It is clear from the circulation estimates and the advertising revenue reported that it is impossible to see the loss-making trend being reversed in the foreseeable future.

5. In the light of paragraphs 2, 3 and 4 above, the Directors must look realistically at the Assets and Liabilities of the Company, and report them immediately to the Board of Trade, and take other appropriate action under the Companies Acts.

6. I submit the following estimate of the State of Affairs of the Company as at today's date, 13th September 1975, after discussion with the Company's Solicitors and Auditors.

ASSETS

Land and Buildings. Value as professionally valued in June 1974, for use other than its present purposes.	£740,000
Plant and Fittings, estimated value realisable on a closure sale, assuming publication of a newspaper is ceased.	100,000
Motor vehicles, estimated realisable value.	25,000
	£865,000
Deduct: HP liabilities in respect of above assets.	22,500
Total of Fixed Assets carried forward.	**£842,500**
Total of Fixed Assets	£842,000

Appendix

Current Assets:		
Stock estimates at 23rd August 1975	£73,500	
Debtors, ditto	268,000	
Investments and Cash, ditto	255,000	
Deduct: provision for 3 weeks losses since these estimates.	60,000	
	£536,500	
Deduct: Prepaid charges included in Debtors, above.	18.000	
	£518,500	
Deduct: Current Liabilities (Creditors) including PAYE etc. Estimates as at 23rd August 1975.	170,000	
		£348,500

Total reserves estimated to be available – carried forward. **£1,190,500**

Total Resources estimated to be available on 13 September 1975. £1,190,500

The Liabilities of the Company, to be met by these Resources are:		
Loans from DTI	£1,200,000	
Loans from Beaverbrook	725,000	
		1,925,000

Estimated Deficiency **£734,500**

7. The only possibility of continuing to trade would be in receiving further assistance in loans, or in grants from DTI.
8. The investment by Shareholders has been lost.
9. As the loan from DTI and £225,000 of the loans from Beaverbrook are secured over the assets of the Company, and as these secured loans exceed the estimated Resources of the Company, ordinary Creditors may not be paid in full, if the estimates of the realisable value of Assets are not exceeded.
10. The Government may feel that it has a duty to the Company in general and to the workforce in particular, in which case the DTI has several options open to it – to abandon its full rights as a secured creditor, to convert its loan into a grant and/or to make further loans.
11. Unless the Government, or some other person or body, is prepared to invest a very substantial amount of further capital in the Company immediately, the Directors have no alternative to winding up its affairs.

WILLIAM WOLFE
Secretary
13 September 1975